RICH FOREVER

Your guarantee to a rich, fulfilling life.

Michael Kendrick

BLUEPRINT
PUBLISHING

richforever.com

Acknowledgements

I would like to thank the many people with whom I have worked to develop the ideas and concepts represented in this book. Especially to Ben Ortlip, an inspired and gifted writer and friend who helped me to articulate the truths that are expressed so eloquently in Rich Forever.

Thank you to all my friends and co-workers at Roswell Capital Partners. Without each of you it would have been impossible to have achieved the success we have in the investment banking business and the platform with which to credibly teach the principles found in this book. Special thanks to my business partner of almost 20 years, Eric Swartz. Eric, thank you for your partnership in business and philanthropy. Your giving spirit is contagious and has been a powerful influence on me all these years.

Thank you to my precious wife and best friend, Michele - the one who truly completes me. Thank you, Michele for your gracious, tender spirit and for displaying God's grace in every place you go.

Thank you to my wonderful children, Grant, Madison and Carson. What joy you each bring to my life. I am so proud of each of you and long to see God reveal himself to you as you grow in your faith.

Thank you Mom and Dad for the loving and faith-filled home which you provided me and the model of Christian faith that you exemplify. Your love and support have been the most precious gift that I have ever received.

Thank you, Boyd Bailey for introducing me to Crown Ministries where I was challenged in my role as a financial steward and for your friendship and the role model that you have provided me during the 12 years that we have been friends.

Thank you to Andy Stanley, my pastor of 15 years whom each week has spoken truth into me and my family at North Point Community Church. Thank you for your leadership and friendship which has significantly shaped my life in so many ways.

And finally thank you to my friends and staff of Blueprint Publishing whose efforts and contributions have made this book possible.

-Michael Kendrick

CONTENTS

Chapter 1

THREE WAYS TO BE RICH

I haven't always wanted to be rich. At least not in the way most people think of rich. As a boy growing up in south Alabama, I didn't get much exposure to people with money. Everybody I knew lived in a basic American house and drove a basic American car. And since the name of our town was Enterprise, I just figured we were about as savvy as it got when it came to those things. I mean, it's not like they named our town Welfare, or Poverty. Sure, I'd seen the Beverly Hillbillies. I knew there was such a thing as becoming a millionaire. But nobody I knew had bubbling crude in their back yard. In my mind, wealth like that only happened to movie stars and oil tycoons. Little did I know how drastically my financial world was about to change.

The little town of Enterprise was home to about 15,000. And frankly, there wasn't much enterprising about it at all. The town square was little more than a spacious intersection where state route 84 intersects College Street. There you can still find the town's famous Boll Weevil monument, recognized as the only monument in the world that honors a pest. Around 1915, the insect destroyed the local cotton business and drove desperate farmers to try peanuts instead. The move was so successful that our county became the largest peanut-producer in the nation within four years. The local economy grew far beyond what it would have been with cotton alone. So they built a monument as a way of saying thanks for the business tip.

Talk about inauspicious beginnings. I literally grew up in a town where the most successful business idea is attributed to an insect.

Most people chuckle when they hear that story. I can hardly say it myself without cracking a smile. But somehow I don't think those farmers meant it as a joke. A disruption like that was serious business. They probably wondered if they'd survive financially. They struggled to put food on the table. They were forced to take risks at a time when they had no business gambling with their family's well-being.

And then, the spectacular happened.

The people of Enterprise went from worst to first. In the game of agriculture, they staged the ultimate comeback. They didn't just survive. They came in first. And I don't think they felt cocky about it either. They had just stared poverty in the face and lived to tell about it. To them, it was probably like a religious experience. At the same time, they kept a sense of humor about it. And in a way, that's the ultimate testimony to their resilience. It didn't break their spirits.

Honestly, I never gave much thought to the name Enterprise, or even their legacy of overcoming adversity. But looking back, I can find parallels to my own story. I've had my share of boll weevil experiences. And I've prospered in ways that can only be considered enterprising. Yet, at the same time, I've never been left feeling cocky about it. Like those farmers, success tends to leave me feeling like something profound just happened, and I'm just grateful I had a good crop. I guess that's the way it is when your successes are balanced by failures. You feel a certain weight of responsibility when you prosper. It makes you think twice before taking credit for an accomplishment. That way, it's pretty hard to take yourself too seriously. It reminds you to have a good laugh about the boll weevils instead of gloating over a bumper crop of peanuts.

If my life were a picture on the wall, then the frame around it would be a simple square made of wood from an old barn or something similar. And then, as luck or providence would have it, when you turn the frame around, the old farmer tucked a winning lottery ticket in back. I'm not saying I didn't work hard to earn my way. It's just that no matter how much I put in, there's always a sense of getting more than I deserve. And while I do believe in a systematic process that is responsible for my success, I consider myself lucky to have stumbled across it in my twenties.

I want you to know these things about my personality because I don't want you to get the wrong picture when I tell you what I have to say about getting rich.

There are lots of people out there writing books and teaching seminars, and they've figured out different ways of getting rich. They flash big money, yachts, and vacation homes to prove they know what they're talking about. And they do know. I'm not saying there's anything wrong with their experiences or the lessons they teach. My concern is that some of the things I'm about to say can sound a little like some of those other guys. But I'm convinced that I'm coming from a completely different place. While my story involves a similar caliber of wealth, I'm not here because I want to dazzle you with dollars. I don't like that approach because it puts too much emphasis in the wrong place. It's misleading. In my case wealth is simply a by-product of what I hope to share in the pages that follow. I hesitate to call it a method, or a process, or a program, or a set of principles, because those terms seem so superficial.

What I learned, and what I want to share with you, goes much deeper. These are some practices that can be incorporated into what you already do. And when they are, I believe they'll reach places and unlock things money can't touch. These principles will not only bring you money, but more importantly, a rich life.

This may be a book about money, but money alone is not the answer to our problems. In fact, money isn't an answer at all. Money is just one of the questions raised by our problems. There are other questions raised too, like how will you spend your time, how will you succeed in marriage and parenting, and how can you have a fulfilling career. Those things are questions, not answers. The practices I want to share with you will put you a lot closer to the answers we all need.

For example, when life raises the money question, it's really asking, "How will you get the things you want?" And without giving it much thought, we say, "If I had the money, I'd just buy them!" And that's how we conclude that money is an answer. We think money would change everything. But money is just a question. It's not an answer. Oh, money changes things, all right. More than we think it will. Sometimes it changes things more than we ever wanted it to. Money brings forces that are both good and bad. Obviously, money can open doors, enable opportunities, and free a person from everyday financial burdens. But money creates a sense of vulnerability that isn't there when you have nothing to lose. Suddenly you have plenty to lose. And that's a stress you'll never know without it.

Money does strange things to relationships too. We think money would improve relationships because it takes away financial pressure that divides people. But big money divides people too. When a couple's bank account is bigger than their love, they don't stand a chance together. This is hard to believe unless you've been through it yourself. It's difficult to imagine two people with tons of money not loving every minute of it. But when money means more to you than the other person, it's just a matter of time before the meltdown. And that's often the tendency when people get rich.

The same thing can happen to your career. Everybody needs fulfilling activities in order to be happy. A career is one of your best bets for finding that kind of fulfillment. Riches, on the other hand, can actually derail a career. After all, the reason most people want to get rich is so that can quit working. But when somebody quits work because they don't need the money, they often cut themselves off from the very thing that was providing them a major source of fulfillment in life. And even if they don't actually quit, they can lose the inner fire that once drove them to expand their limits and reach their potential.

So there has to be something more. Money alone can't answer the real questions life raises. Questions simply can't do that. Only answers can.

That's why I think it's so important to understand that I'm not simply talking about a plan to accumulate wealth, even though I believe you will almost certainly experience financial improvement when you utilize these practices. If you somehow conclude that it's about the money, you'll discard the most valuable part. That's like settling for a diamond when you could have owned the mine.

These practices that I discovered have not only answered the money question, but also the relationship question, the time question, the career question, and so on. The answer to virtually any version of the "How will I get what I want" question can be found in them. Once I adopted them as my own, I became more adventurous and more focused. Because of them, I developed the ability to see three or four moves ahead as I navigate through life. They have led me to accomplish things I'd never dreamed of as a boy. It's been like possessing a virtual blueprint to follow for any category of life I wished to improve – relationships, career, fitness, and of course, finances.

> There are three different ways to be rich. And if you aren't rich in all three, then you aren't really rich at all.

I've come to the conclusion that a person's not truly rich unless he's rich in all these categories. That's what it looks like to own the diamond and the mine. Needless to say, I haven't always understood this. Over the years, my definition of "rich" has undergone dozens of renovations. So before I share my plan for getting rich, I should explain exactly what I mean by "rich". Because I actually think there are three different ways to be rich. And if you aren't rich in all three, then you aren't really rich at all.

Looking back, I was already rich in the days of my childhood. I didn't have much in the way of cash or assets. But I had many of the things we all want deep down inside. I had a great family, plenty of friends, and a nice community to explore. Most of all, I was raised with a basic sense that I had a purpose in the world. Not that I had to go make something happen in order to matter. I was taught that everyone has value inherently, regardless of what you accomplish. In an environment like that, it's not hard to feel good about yourself. And that's the kind of wealth money can't buy.

As a result, I never felt like I was missing much. So while I wasn't against the idea of making a lot of money someday, the truth is I wasn't doing too bad without it. That's the thing about this topic of being rich. It's like a riddle. On one hand, money seems really important, but on the other hand money can't seem to buy the really important things. Throughout my financial journey, I've come face to face with this puzzling reality over and over. One minute, money makes the world go 'round. The next

> On one hand, money seems really important, but on the other hand money can't seem to buy the really important things.

minute, you can't stop the world with any amount of money. Maybe it's been part of my purpose in the world to live through those ups and downs. At any rate, I was not only destined to make lots of money, but also to learn some important lessons about riches. To this day, I'm at a loss to say which is more valuable, the money or the lessons. Actually, I kind of like having both.

When it comes to the word "rich", I recognize three important ways it needs to be defined. I've experienced two of these three during my lifetime, and I'm working on the third every day. In the pages that follow, I'd like to describe these three definitions of rich in more detail.

As you already know, the first meaning speaks to financial riches. I'll stop short of saying I've mastered that one, but from the time I started applying these practices, my net worth grew beyond the point of meeting all my income needs or desires. Ever since, my biggest financial problems have been in the category of how to manage excess wealth. I will spend several chapters describing the techniques responsible for my financial successes. And I will teach you the practices that you can apply to your own life.

The second meaning of rich is also evident by now. Becoming rich in the area of fulfillment is an art form in itself. Once you have money, how can you be sure it won't destroy you? How can you be sure you'll actually enjoy your relationships, your work, and the way you spend your time? For that matter, how can you experience maximum fulfillment in those areas even when you don't have money? Surprisingly, the same techniques that made me rich financially are responsible for the wealth I've known in this second category. Behind the pursuit of money itself is a simple, practical approach that can bring about prosperity in other areas. I'll spend some time describing my own journey to this second dimension of wealth, and I'll explain in detail how you can begin right away to experience the same kind of fulfillment in your life.

Finally, I'll explain what I mean by the third type of rich. In many ways, it's the most important one. And as you can guess, it's the last one we normally think about. Yet, it is recognized by business and cultural leaders as an essential part of the foundation of any civilization. Philosophers and writers have acknowledged its importance since ancient times. But despite its prominence in the back of our minds, without a deliberate strategy for it, you and I would likely wake up one day in utter poverty in this category.

That's my road map for the pages that follow. And I truly believe that if you'll walk with me through this process, you'll not only find yourself in a new place financially, you'll find your life completely fulfilling and you can actually be rich forever.

Chapter 2

MAYONNAISE AND CRACKERS

I once heard a financial adviser make a peculiar prediction. He said that if you took all the money away from the rich people and gave it to the poor people, an amazing thing would happen in about five years. He said that when it all played out, all the rich people would have found a way to get their wealth back, and all the poor people would have somehow parted ways with the millions they'd been given. In other words, becoming rich isn't so much about the *becoming* part. It has more to do with your ability to *be* rich in the first place.

If you think about it, there's a lot of truth to that prediction. When most of us think about getting rich some day, our minds run to how to get that way, or what it would be like once we do. But we don't give much thought to the kind of mentality it takes to create wealth in the first place. And that's why most people fail. It's hard to create what you don't understand. The reason most people lose money, or fail to acquire it in the first place, is that they don't understand how money works – where it comes from, why it grows, and where it goes when it leaves. So even if you win the lottery some day, if you don't have a basic understanding of money, your relationship with it will be short-lived at best.

Wealth is not about being financially set. It's about having a mind set. If your mind is in the right place, the money will follow. Not to mention, it will stay too. So rather than telling you what to *do* to get rich, my goal is to teach you how to *think* to get rich. And once you are wealthy, how to stay that way.

> **My goal is to teach you how to *think* to get rich, and once you are wealthy, how to stay that way.**

The first major lesson I learned on this subject came during the summer of 1979. I'd always had a knack for generating spending money when I needed it. When I was fourteen, I got a paper route so I could buy cold sodas at the corner store, as well as gas for my mini-bike. When I finally reached the employable age of sixteen, I quickly applied for a bag boy position at the grocery store, where a boy could earn $3.25 an hour. That was big money to me. Needless to say, it didn't take much to keep me going back in those days. Quite predictably, my earnings tended to track pretty closely with my entertainment budget. My perspective on work and money was simple. When you want something, just work a little, then buy it.

Frankly, that philosophy works fine when your only goal in life is to keep twenty dollars in your pocket. But the minute you set your sights on the things of adulthood, the greater uses of money are revealed.

That's what happened to me in 1979. After one year at the nearby Junior College, I was ready to stretch my nineteen year old wings. I'd conquered all there was to conquer in Enterprise, and I was ready for the next challenge. My goal? It was to make it on my own in the resort town of Fort Meyers, FL with my buddy Ricky. I guess the seed was planted in my head when Ricky moved down there to stay with his brother. He found a job delivering welding canisters to construction sites and suddenly Ricky seemed to me like an adventurous pioneer with a plot of fertile land and a pan full of gold. Every day I remained at home left me further and further behind in the race to explore the frontier. I threw together a plan and within a few weeks I packed my car and headed off to join my friend.

The naivety of my vision was immediately obvious in the eyes of Ricky's brother, who was less than thrilled now that there were *two* teenagers sharing his apartment and freeloading off his graces. So as soon as I could find a job, Ricky and I got a place of our own and moved in.

At first, we were living the life. My father had given me two hundred dollars and a tank of gas to get me going, so I felt like the new rich kid in town. On top of that, I was now getting paid to drive a delivery truck for a building supply company, and my first three-figure paycheck was just days away. Living on my own was even more satisfying than I had imagined. There was nobody to tell me what to do or when to do it. I had my own apartment, my own car, and my own job. And best of all, I had my own choices. When work was over, I could go wherever I wanted and be whoever I wanted to be.

The freedom was so intoxicating that I didn't even mind the painful working conditions awaiting me each morning. I used to think south Alabama was hot until I spent the summer in south Florida in a truck with no air conditioning. When most people experience Florida, they're either sitting by a pool or splashing in the waves between naps on a beach blanket. And even when there's a coastal breeze and you're wearing nothing but a bathing suit, it's still hot. But there's a big difference when you're dressed for manual labor in the sweltering Florida sun.

For starters, you begin sweating the minute you step out of the shower in the morning. As a result, you never quite get all the way dry. Then, before the sun's all the way up, you're loading the truck with cast iron tubs, cinder blocks, lumber, bags of concrete, or PVC pipe. The dirt and dust from those materials mix with sweat to form a wet blanket of insulation over every square inch of your body. The unique design allows heat from the sun to come in, but it prevents any from escaping. To make matters worse, almost every delivery stop involves unloading materials and stacking them on dusty makeshift shelves inside a tin shed with no windows. When you open the doors on one of those hothouses, the heat that's been building up all day rushes out like sparks from a blast furnace. It's enough to singe your eyebrows. Despite the hostility of this environment, it seems to be the habitat of choice for the entire spider and snake population.

By the end of the day, you feel drained, dried, and sapped. The overwhelming desire to collapse on the bed is surpassed only by the need to cool off, re-hydrate, shower, and feed your ravenous appetite.

Once those basic needs are met, your body seems to slip into unconsciousness until the alarm clock wakes you to start it all over again.

Fortunately for me, I was no stranger to hard work. From as early as I can remember, my father kept me attached to his hip while he worked the little farm where we lived. His day job was repairing helicopter avionics at the military base. He'd get up around five in the morning and put in eight hours by two or three o'clock in the afternoon. When he got home, he didn't stop to catch his breath before cranking up the tiller or jumping on the tractor. He'd stay at it until dark almost every day. And in the summer months, that meant nine o'clock or later. Most of that time, he made sure I was riding in his lap or walking right by his side. He'd put me to work at whatever task made sense for my young age. I shucked corn, strung beans, and pulled weeds. When I was old enough to push a lawn mower, he had me cutting grass at our house, my granny's house, and even the lawn at the church. I was responsible for so much grass each week that it was literally time to start cutting again by the time I'd finished mowing it all.

Between my dad's example and my own experience with work growing up, I had the ability to labor just about as hard as anyone without crumpling under the weight of it. So when I say it was hard work driving that delivery truck, it's not like when an old lady complains about a flight of stairs or a third-grader whines about making the bed. If the concept of work had been my primary object lesson that summer, I would have graduated at the top of my class. But as challenging as my job was, it was nothing compared to the challenge I faced in the area of handling finances.

Like I said before, my earnings had always tracked pretty close to my entertainment budget. So when I got out on my own with Ricky, I fell naturally into the same pattern. I was earning like never before, and so my tendency was to entertain like never before too. You see, in my eyes the value of a dollar was limited to its potential for entertainment. Up to that point in my life, I'd never witnessed its value in any other arena. Sure, I understood that it could buy all kinds of different things. But the only need I'd ever seen money meet was the little stuff a kid from Enterprise wants. All the rest was just intellectual theory.

Both Ricky and I would get our paychecks every two weeks. And for the first week or so, things were looking up. We each paid our portion of the rent and utilities. We bought gas, groceries, and clothes. For ten out of fourteen days, we lived like sultans. But on about the eleventh day of every cycle, a strange transformation would take place. The pantry became an empty closet. The refrigerator morphed into an oversized ice-maker. And the sultans were demoted to peasants in their own kingdom. Needless to say, our wallets turned into glorified driver's license holders.

When the money ran out, we did what most short-sighted bachelors do. We resorted to scraping together meals from the condiments and dry goods that accumulate in even the sparsest of kitchens. In our case, we made sandwiches consisting of nothing more than two dry crackers held together with a layer of mayonnaise. I remember surviving for stretches of two or three days on that same meager menu as we counted down the hours until the next paycheck.

I wish I could say that we only reached that point of desperation once. But in our case, the cycle kept repeating itself over and over again.

By the end of that summer, I'd had enough. My fledgling fantasy of freedom had been systematically smashed against the rocks of reality. I'd had enough of mayonnaise and crackers. All my paradigms about making it on my own were up for grabs again. And I headed back home to Enterprise, Alabama to rethink the game plan.

Needless to say, that was a defining moment for me. The lessons I brought back home were like the pavers of a new foundation on which I was destined to build my life. I was starting to learn the meaning of responsibility. I had a deeper understanding of the value of a dollar. But perhaps more importantly, I saw that life was a school with classes forming daily. In my quest to catch a fish, I had accidentally discovered that fishing was a craft that might feed me for a lifetime. And the greatest principle I learned about money was the sheer fact that money had principles. Furthermore, if I could somehow master these principles, or even begin to wrestle them, I might leverage them for as much upside as I had unwittingly done for downside. It wasn't that I detested eating mayonnaise and crackers. I was developing a taste for the raw potential that exists in a simple financial vision. For starters, I finally had a *felt* need for money that went beyond just entertainment. I had gotten a taste – literally – of the value of money to feed, clothe, and provide other basic necessities. And with that revelation, I was suddenly alerted to the idea that there might be other important lessons to be learned about money as

> **The greatest principle I learned about money was the sheer fact that money had principles.**

well. And if it meant avoiding starvation and failure, I was interested in hearing more about it.

You see, it's just like that financial advisor said. If you had given me a million dollars back then, I would have quickly lost it. I not only lacked the mentality to acquire it, I lacked the mentality to keep it. And that was just the tip of the iceberg. My first leap from the nest had been quite a nosedive. I'd felt the rush of the wind across my spread wings, but it was mostly an exercise in the law of gravity, not the laws of aerodynamics. I had a lot to learn if I ever wanted to fly.

But something was changing inside me now. A switch had been flipped. I didn't have all the answers yet. But I was on a quest. Not only had I been awakened to the urgency of making ends meet, I was somehow alerted to a whole category of financial concepts that were waiting to be discovered. Like a kid in his father's shop, I'd played around with a very powerful tool and gotten injured. And I came away thinking that anything that powerful, if used wisely, would be a mighty handy addition to my toolbox someday.

On the practical side, there's something about feeling your back against the wall that wakes you up to reality. Thanks to my upbringing, I had been more prepared for hard work than anyone I knew. And now, working harder than ever, I couldn't even make a month's pay last three weeks. Something needed to change. How would I ever be able to afford my next car, or my own house, or retirement? Clearly, there was more to the equation than hard work alone.

You can talk to a child about the value of a good education, or acquiring marketable skills for a career. But none of that compares to the impact of learning it first hand. We may think with our brains, but we truly learn with our stomachs. When your very existence is at stake, suddenly you can find the willpower and motivation to learn anything.

That's what I brought back home to Enterprise at the end of the summer. I'd set out to make a living. And now I was coming home ready to make a life.

If that delivery job in south Florida was the best I could do without a college degree, then I was willing to reevaluate my decision to abandon a formal education. So I not only re-enrolled in the junior college, but I made plans to enter the aerospace engineering program at Auburn University when I was finished.

In short, Lesson 1 simply taught me that there were lessons. If I didn't learn them, I would suffer. And maybe, just maybe, if I set my mind to learn them I could prosper.

And little did I know how quickly I'd prosper. Because in just a few short years I'd be a high-flying executive being groomed to set the world on fire.

Chapter 3

STRAPPING ON ROCKETS

I returned home to Enterprise the way a space ship comes back to earth. It was as if the young man who had rocketed out of town just a few weeks before had been burned up on re-entry. Only the command module remained. I was coming home strained and stretched, and bringing back new findings that would change my understanding of the world. I would never be the same.

My mission to Fort Meyers hadn't gone anything like I'd expected. But somehow, the result was even more valuable because of it. That's the thing about exploration. The objective you set out to accomplish might never quite materialize, but in its place you discover something even bigger. As I think back, I'm not so sure my mission on that trip was to start a new life in Florida. Whether I had known it or not, in the back of my mind I had simply been on a mission to go exploring. Deep inside, I think I just wanted to know what was out there in the world. And moving south with Ricky was just my subconscious way of pursuing my true cause. Outwardly, the mission had failed. But inwardly, I discovered many things. And that success easily overshadowed the obvious failures. It had cost me a few hundred dollars and a little discomfort. But that's a small price to pay for a vision that would change my life. I think I could already sense that the insight I'd gained was going to be valuable. But I had no idea that it was about to produce a return of a million dollars, then tens of millions, and eventually hundreds of millions.

That's the second lesson I want to present here: Nothing is a failure when it leads to something else. In other words, failure is a word used by people who don't bother sifting through the wreckage for parts that can be salvaged. Or, as Thomas Edison said, "Many of life's failures are people who did not realize how close they were to success when they gave up."

> "Many of life's failures are people who did not realize how close they were to success when they gave up."
> -Thomas Edison

Of course at that point in life, the thought of giving up never crossed my mind. I still had my whole life ahead of me, and plenty of cards I hadn't played yet. But the experience helps me remember this principle of leveraging failure. And it would turn out to be a lesson that I would come back to over and over again later in life. It's a good thing I didn't forget it. Because some of the failures I experienced later were the kind that prompt men to jump from bridges.

I think the key to pushing through failure has little to do with keeping a "positive" attitude or remembering a famous quotation like Thomas Edison's. Those superficial techniques are little comfort when the boll weevils eat your cotton crop. No, the real key to seeing past your failures is to set your eyes beyond them in the first place. In fact, it's best to look so far ahead that you're open to a variety of possible outcomes in the short term. That way, you don't set yourself up for devastation when your one and only plan doesn't pan out. Like I said, the real goal of my heart during that summer in Florida hadn't been to make it on my own. It was all just an excuse to explore the world. I was looking for multiple possibilities. In many ways, I succeeded before I even reached Tallahassee.

> The real key to seeing past your failures is to set your eyes beyond them in the first place.

In contrast, imagine if I'd really had my heart set on the single outcome of finding the perfect life in Florida. What if I'd somehow imagined that I was going to land the perfect job, buy the perfect house, find the perfect wife, and raise the perfect family? My hopes would have been attached to a number of short-term results. Imagine how devastating it would have been to admit that none of my goals had been attained. It would have felt like my whole life was over. I might as well drag myself back to Enterprise and dig my own grave right there next to Aunt Flossie.

I'm not sure who to thank for instilling that outlook in me at such an early age. Maybe it was my parents, or my kindergarten teacher.

Or maybe it was pure luck. But looking back, I consider it one of the most important lessons I've ever known. As long as you keep your mind open to multiple short-term outcomes, with a long-term vision in mind, you'll always have the notion to pick yourself up and dust yourself off and move on. But the minute you bet everything on one horse, you run the risk of going bust.

Of course I'm not saying we shouldn't have specific goals. In the pages that follow, you'll see how incredibly detailed some of my goals have been. However, behind the best goals you'll always find a deeper value – something that can be served through a wide variety of options and outcomes. Values can remain intact no matter what happens. But circumstances come and go. So even in the case of specific goals, it's the value behind it that keeps you going. The goal is just a milestone used to mark your progress toward a larger objective – one that is grounded in a value, in a life purpose.

Nobody flies without a flight plan. The human soul has a need to know where it's going. Whether you're talking about your career, family plans, or your life purpose in general, we must have a general picture of where we're headed. Even Aristotle noted, "The soul never thinks without a picture." That's what vision is. It's a mental picture of where this all leads. And what I would add to the equation is that your vision needs to be larger than the moment you're in. If the vision lives or dies based on a single moment or a particular set of circumstances, then you'll experience failure eventually. And when you do, it will seem like total failure. It

> **Your vision needs to be larger than the moment you're in.**

will wear away at your will to live, and weaken your sense of motivation.

But when your mindset is focused on the long-term, there's really no such thing as failure. It's all just one big exploratory mission, and you're simply mapping out the options that lead to the ultimate vision, and ruling out the ones that don't.

> **When your mindset is focused on the long-term, there's really no such thing as failure.**

Most importantly, when your eyes stay on the horizon like that, you never run out of motivation. The basic sense of momentum remains steady, despite the occasional setbacks and dead-ends. And every experience, whether good or bad, provides important data that informs your future choices and shapes your life.

On my journey to explore the world, I had discovered a no-man's land that I wanted to avoid in the future. I had ventured into a place where my education and training were insufficient for the kind of lifestyle I needed. So I made a note on my mental roadmap never to go there again. Suddenly, going to school was not just something to endure because my parents said I ought to. Continuing my education was a natural part of the journey that would ensure I never went through that no-man's land again. My general vision for my life hadn't changed much, I was just fine-tuning the route.

So with that backdrop of logic formulating in my subconscious, I returned home to Enterprise and quickly completed junior college. Not only that, I made straight A's. I'd never been a good student before. I guess I hadn't seen the point in it. Or I had other priorities. But now I had traveled some of the roads reserved for C and D students. Those roads were hot. They were difficult. And there wasn't much to eat. I wanted a different road to travel. I wanted a wider road with more lanes. I wanted exits with plenty of restaurants and other excursions. I wanted to be on the kind of roads the A students traveled. And that little bit of clarity was all it took to transform my identity in the classroom. In fact, I did become an A student. I moved straight to the top of the class and stayed there until graduation.

At the end of junior college, I signed up for the Aerospace Engineering program at Auburn University. I chose Aerospace Engineering because I'd always enjoyed math and I figured rockets were the fastest way to get wherever I was going.

With my aerospace engineering degree in hand, I quickly landed a job with Pratt & Whitney Aircraft in West Palm Beach, FL. Just a few summers ago, I was driving that truck in Fort Meyers, and now I landed a job designing fighter jets! The pay was great. And the air-conditioned offices would be even better. And the prestige was nice too. Imagine the response when I told people that my new job was developing the most advanced aircraft in the world.

So with all those great things going for me, I never expected to be looking for a new career from the moment I walked in on my first day. What in the world would cause me to jump ship so quickly, at least mentally? Why in the world would I ever want to leave such an ideal situation, especially when you consider the job I took next?! Well, I need to explain what I was thinking when I accepted that job in the first place.

For the most part, my life was heading in the right direction. I'd worked out my motivation issues. I managed to create some goals for my education and career. And I was learning how to achieve my objectives with success. But despite these great leaps, I still had a few things to learn about vision. Keeping your eyes fixed on a distant horizon does not make up for having fuzzy vision. The thing you're aiming for may be a long way off. But it still needs to be clear.

I believed in where I was going and in how to get there. And I was accelerating rapidly along the course that would get me there. The problem, however, was that my vision needed refining. Up to this point, I had only decided that I wanted to be successful. But I hadn't gone the next step to define what success looks like for me. I didn't need to know everything. But I needed a few milestones. And since I didn't clarify them up front – or couldn't clarify them yet – I was about to find out the hard way.

Success was a very important value to me. My short stay in Fort Myers confirmed that. In that one summer, I stood at the crossroads between two paths. One led to a life of financial struggle and hardship – something less than what I considered to be success. The other had the potential to take me to higher-paying jobs and work that was more fulfilling – my idea of success. In essence, I read the compass for the first time and learned north from south. But so far, that's all I knew.

In the years that followed, I was destined to learn that there's much more to navigating the road to success than knowing up from down. You can't get there just by running full speed in one direction versus another. As you start to get close, there are turns to be made, and angles of attack to consider. In addition to shooting for a point in the distance, I needed to fill in some lines in the middle of my map.

Because, as it turned out, success wasn't the only value important to me. I wanted a certain type of success – one that included two other distinctions that I valued almost as much.

First, I had a nagging fear of normalcy. My parents did government work throughout their careers. In my eyes they have been extraordinarily successful people. But after growing up around Uncle Sam's way of running things, I was left with an ambition to work in a different system. In order to fulfill my own definition of success, I wanted a life that was outside your typical institutions. Maybe everybody feels that way. And maybe we all have our different ways of accomplishing just that. But I had this idea that I wanted to break away from the 9 to 5. And that leads to the second distinction for my vision: I wanted to achieve autonomy. In other words, I wanted the freedom to pursue life independent of any obligation to a company or a paycheck. Essentially, I wanted a net worth sufficient to fund all my dreams, and a schedule capable of accommodating them.

Unfortunately, I hadn't quite put my finger on all these details when I signed up for aerospace… or even by the time I entered the work force. But they made themselves obvious on my very first day on the job. And that brings us back to the moment I realized I needed to change careers.

I wouldn't go so far as to say the division where I reported was a cubicle farm. But there was something about it that reeked of predictability. And in my mind, it represented the kind of normalcy I had vowed to escape in response to my parents' careers. As I looked across the office where I worked, I could practically mark out the years in cubicles. My cube represented year one – entry level. Eleven feet away, my boss's cube represented the twenty year mark. And seventeen feet beyond that, my boss's boss sat at the thirty-year mark.

The rest of my life was to be a twenty-eight foot journey from a small cubicle to a medium one to a large one. No matter how hard I worked, or how much I accomplished, I would never go any farther in life than twenty-eight feet. It was almost morbid. And it was more than I could bear.

I didn't know the words for what I was feeling. I didn't understand that I was clarifying my vision, or fine-tuning my definition of success. All I knew is that *being the best you can be* was over-rated. Sure, it was important. But it wasn't sufficient.

Not knowing what else to do, I reached even higher. If being my best hadn't been enough, then maybe I needed to be the *bestest* I could be. So within a week, I enrolled in the MBA program at Embry-Riddle Aeronautical University and began planning my escape. For nearly three years, I designed engines by day and studied business by night. I wasn't sure where it would take me. As long as it took me away from there.

It's funny how the human mind works. One minute I'm ambling through life with no particular ambition in mind. The next, I'm rocketing along so fast that I'm starting to get ahead of myself. In one short season of life I had gone from no ambition to blind ambition. I don't mean to sound like I regret any of these steps. I believe each one has been an important part of my journey. It's just that there are some intriguing lessons in human behavior to be gleaned here.

First we learn the importance of doing something.

> First we learn the importance of doing something. Then we learn the importance of doing something important.

Then we learn the importance of doing something important.

I don't know why it's not obvious to us sooner. It seems we could save ourselves some effort if we gave as much attention to *what* we're doing as we do *how much* or *how fast* we're doing it. Today, I call it being intentional. But it would be several job changes before I finally put a name to it.

The MBA was supposed to be my ticket into the business side of technology. I still had a technical mind, but I had discovered that pure engineering wasn't for me. So now I was an engineer with an MBA. Surely that would make me more attractive. But as I eventually discovered, there was still a glaring omission to my resume. I had no business or sales experience. And that would prevent me from making the short list with the companies I was pursuing.

Thankfully, I had something more influential than sales experience. I had a friend named Dennis. I'd met Dennis at the same church where I met my wife, Michele. Dennis was sharp-dressed and well-spoken. He looked like the cover of GQ magazine. More importantly, he just happened to be a district manager with Lanier Copiers. So when he offered me a sales position, I jumped on it. And even though copier sales was hard work, at least I would be compensated for my effort. Perhaps more importantly, I would get a chance to prove some new abilities.

The new job was a big change with some serious trade-offs. One day I was designing jet fighters, the next day I was pulling a copier down the street and getting doors slammed in my face. And when I called my mom and dad to tell them about my new position, they were shocked. "How could you throw five years of engineering school down the drain to go sell copiers?" It wasn't easy to explain, but I convinced them it was part of my master plan to take a step back in order to take two steps forward. I needed to prove to the world that I could sell something. By doing so, I would distance myself from the stereotypes of propeller-head engineers that thrive behind a computer screen in a cubicle. I had to prove I had drive and personality if I was ever going to get my foot in the lucrative door of high-tech sales.

I thought delivering plumbing supplies had been hard, but I hadn't seen anything yet. Try loading up a van full of copiers every morning at eight o'clock in a suit and tie. The muggy air in West Palm Beach feels like soaking in a hot tub fully clothed. And if the physical challenge wasn't enough, this job added a mental challenge to boot. Each day, we were required to make fifty walk-in cold-calls before lunch! That's right, by noon. Now, you may be wondering how it's mathematically possible to make that many cold calls in person in just half a day. Those would be solid numbers over the phone, much less adding all the driving and walking too. Well, consider that 80% of the prospects kicked us out in five to ten seconds and you start to see how. Some of them even offered a little shove to help us make up lost time. Talk about an assault on your self-esteem! The rejection was unbearable. At the end of my first day on the job, I just sat in my van and sobbed. What had I done? I never expected sales to be this hard. And to do this day after day would be intolerable.

Before long, I mustered a little sales magic and figured out how to get past the receptionist to the office manager. And after many days of empty cold calls, I made my first sale of a $1500 copier. I'd finally broken the ice. The $150 commission wasn't much, but the confidence it birthed was invaluable. Gradually, I got better and better at deflecting the rejection and knifing my way through to the people who were ready to buy. My closing ratio improved so much I ended my first year as one of the top copier salesmen in the South Florida district. My first year out as a salesman, I earned $60,000 – quite a jump from the $35,000 I was making as an aerospace engineer.

The next three years turned out to be my real-life MBA as I steadily climbed the ladder to success. That experience taught me several important lessons. I learned what it felt like to humble yourself in order to achieve a goal. I learned that often in life you have to take a step back in order to move forward. And that to pursue a long-term vision, there are short-term sacrifices. I also found out that cold-calling is really hard!

> **To pursue a long-term vision, there are short-term sacrifices.**

My accomplishments at Lanier were a springboard into an exclusive program with Lanier's parent company, Harris Corporation. The program was called "WINGS" and it was designed specifically for engineers with an MBA. True to its name, it was a high-flying incubator for fast-tracking super-achievers. Those of us in the program were being groomed for development. They taught us how to dress and speak, how to achieve, and how to be leaders. They threw parties for us around the country where we rubbed elbows with upper management. The perks and privileges helped instill a sense of confidence that complemented the arsenal of skills they were teaching us. By the time we emerged from the WINGS program, we were lean mean selling machines.

If selling copiers had been the ego-downer, the WINGS program was the ego-booster. At times I had to pinch myself. I couldn't believe what they were allowing a 26 year old small-town kid from Alabama to do. I was jetting all over the country representing Harris Corporation – a $2 Billion aerospace company – negotiating defense contracts worth tens and sometimes hundreds of millions of dollars. There were times I was sitting down in the offices of the Pentagon discussing spaced-based lasers and the like with Air Force colonels. Wow. I'd come a long way in just 7 years – from recent high school graduate driving a sweltering delivery truck in South Florida and surviving on mayonnaise and crackers until payday.

And then it happened.

Just when I thought I had reached the top, I stumbled across the secret formula… the Holy Grail… the Matrix. I wasn't looking for it. It just happened. Although it wasn't obvious right away, it would become the game-changer for me. Using what I had stumbled upon would create for me financial wealth greater than anything I had dreamed.

> **Using what I had stumbled upon would create for me financial wealth greater than anything I had dreamed.**

Chapter 4

BLUEPRINT FOR LIFE

What I'm about to explain is nothing short of the secret to my success. If there's one thing responsible for putting me where I am today, this is it. But within that context, if I had to name one factor that was the most significant point of leverage in my life, there's no question about it. Before discovering this secret, I was a reasonably accomplished guy. Without a doubt, I was on my way up the ladder at a pace well ahead of my peers. If you had assessed my potential – my intelligence, my level of ambition, and my network of opportunities – you would have concluded that I had become everything I was capable of becoming. I had achieved significant success for a 26 year old.

But what happened next was an eye-opener that changed everything. And it really felt like I'd found the secret to success.

I call it a secret for good reason. First of all, because I just don't hear many people talking about it. It's the simplest thing in the world. And if you know where to look, you'll see that many of the world's most successful people swear by it. Still, you hardly ever hear it mentioned in the normal walks of life. It's not mentioned on the news, or in casual conversation. But dig behind the scenes of the top achievers in the world and it's there in one form or another. I'm not sure why it doesn't get more attention. It's as vital as the air we breathe. At any rate, it remains a secret to most.

Second, I guess it doesn't get headlines because there's an element of the unexplained to it. I'm not even sure you'll be able to grasp it after reading my description. I mean, it all seems practical and basic. But when you claim that it's the difference between a net worth of a few hundred thousand versus tens of millions, it can seem like a stretch. And yet, if I had to put a dollar figure on it, I'd have to say that's the impact it's had for me.

Its influence is not just financial either. It's been my experience that this one factor has the ability to shape virtually any aspect of a person's life. I've applied these concepts in the area of relationships, in business, in parenting, and physical fitness.

As I've mentioned, there's a part of me that feels funny giving such a strong endorsement to something so elusive and intangible. I can't help wondering if I'm starting to sound like a late-night infomercial that promises to change your life for just $19.95. At the same time, I don't want to be guilty of underemphasizing this factor either. Where most "breakthroughs" might take you from a 7 to a 9 (on a scale of 1-10), this one necessitated resetting my dials so they go to 100. Literally.

I'll admit, I've often seen similar endorsements made by guys who were either after money, or a moment of fame, or who-knows-what. In light of their motives, I never saw past their hucksterism long enough to consider what they were pitching. At any rate, if my description starts to raise red flags like that, just keep in mind that I'm only sharing my personal experience. If I were motivated by money, I wouldn't seek it by trying to become an author. And as far as fame goes, I'm really not the type that enjoys putting himself in the spotlight. But I am a guy who feels a burden of responsibility to share what I've been given in life, whether it's monetary wealth or a set of techniques to help people reach their goals. In fact, I'd be satisfied to see these principles finally presented without the shady air of suspicion that has helped to keep them obscured all these years.

So with that set of disclaimers as the backdrop, here's the story of my introduction to this next dimension in the universe of success.

When I worked for Harris, I was traveling all over the country, spending a lot of time in airports and in the air. My exposure to my company's executive grooming process sparked my interest in literature about business and personal development. So during my time on the road, I began to browse the kinds of books that explored those things. Many of the things I read were attempts to introduce new buzzwords for business or present a revolutionary school of thought for the economy. Others dealt with techniques for maximizing productivity or balancing responsibilities.

Inevitably, I happened across one that stood out from the rest. I don't even want to mention the title here because that's not the point. In fact, my main take-away from the book wasn't exactly the author's primary message. But in the process of presenting his ideas, the author touched on something that I'd never considered before.

In the months and years to follow, I would discover a number of books and other writings that packaged the same concepts in various forms. In some cases, they came straight from the greatest thinkers of our time. Based on what I know now, I can say that these principles first appeared in some of the oldest writings known to man.

> The Law of Intentionality says that when you declare your intent consciously, your subconscious gets busy contributing to your consciously stated goal.

The basic idea, whenever it has been mentioned, is a concept I call intentionality. In essence, it says that your brain has two ways of functioning. The first is conscious function. And the other is subconscious. My own Law of Intentionality simply suggests that whenever you declare your intent consciously, your subconscious gets busy contributing to your consciously stated goal.

For example, let's say I'm considering the purchase of a red Jeep automobile. I might research several on the Internet. I'll probably test drive some at a local dealership. I'll take home the brochures and pour over the pictures. Over the course of several days or weeks I declare a conscious intent to heighten my awareness of anything related to that particular vehicle. I become intentional about it.

Meanwhile, my subconscious mind looks for ways to play a supporting role in whatever I'm doing. That's its purpose. Like a computer that processes data in the background, the subconscious services important tasks that exceed the bandwidth of your conscious mind's one-track limitation. This explains how you can walk from one room to the next without having to concentrate on balance or stride length. And it's the reason you don't forget to breathe every 3-5 seconds, even though it's not top-of-mind. Your subconscious mind maintains a plethora of important processes at any given time.

So when it begins to sense my new emphasis on a red Jeep, it allocates a measure of bandwidth for searching and processing any data related to the subject. And sure enough, when I'm surrounded by hundreds of cars on the way to work the next day, guess which one I notice ahead of me and several lanes over. You guessed it. Even though I can barely make it out behind the tractor-trailer rig, my attention goes right to it. And here's the thing: I wasn't even thinking about cars at the time. I was deep in thought about a meeting, or a family outing, or an old friend I haven't seen since childhood. Regardless, my subconscious located this vehicle and brought it to my attention as if to give me one more perspective to consider for my purchasing decision.

Have you ever had an experience like that?

Have you ever racked your brain over a situation only to have the solution pop into your head with relative ease when you least expect it? Or have you ever been presented with a complicated situation that left you feeling the need to come back to it later? When you call a time-out for your conscious mind like that, it doesn't always mean your subconscious stops working on it. Oftentimes, your request to "mull it over" or "think about it" or "sleep on it" is nothing more than an announcement of your intention to turn it over to your subconscious processing power.

This practice of allowing our thoughts to gel is as familiar as vegging out in front of the television or stepping out for some fresh air.

So far, this is nothing more than Psychology 101. But here's where the road forks for most of us, and you either go one direction or the other. Obviously, the authors I read didn't stop with a basic lesson in psychology. They went on to speculate about the power of the subconscious mind to process thoughts in the background. Depending on the source, they usually suggest specific tasks that can leverage the resources of the subconscious. They tell amazing stories to wow their audiences and back up their claims. And I think this is where they begin to lose mainstream credibility. In an effort to convince their skeptics, they resort to more and more extreme examples to make their point. As a result, their fantastical examples and impassioned monologues end up making them sound a little too much like an illusionist from a Vaudevillian sideshow. By using terms like "channeling" and "tapping into", they make the subconscious function of the brain sound like paranormal activity. And when it starts to sound like a ghost story, most people dismiss it as a fairy tale and tune out.

To shroud the subject even further, there's the whole Freudian movement of the 50s and 60s, which was responsible for popularizing terms like "subconscious" with most of us in the first place. Thanks to that connotation, we can hardly hear those words without conjuring cartoon images of a pipe-smoking therapist spouting unintelligible psychobabble.

In the end, there are plenty of factors to dissuade us from taking this subject very seriously or exploring its useful potential.

If it hadn't been for the timing when I happened across it, I don't think I would have been as open as I was. My employer at the time was a veritable factory for future executives. After experiencing one of their makeovers firsthand, I was pretty ripe for the topic of pushing the limits of one's potential. In almost any other chapter of my life, I might have scoffed and looked for more practical conversations. But I was tolerant enough of the idiosyncrasies to search for the truth in what those guys were saying. Maybe they couldn't quite put their finger on it, but there was something there.

By the time I finished the first book, I was convinced of several things. First, I believed it was possible to make better use of my subconscious mind to support my conscious goals and intentions. I didn't know how. But it was possible. Second, I knew that my expectations from life had always been formed around my conscious abilities, without factoring in my potential if my subconscious carried a portion of the load. And finally, I concluded that if I could create more of a connection between my conscious and subconscious, my expectations of life would change significantly. In other words, I could supercharge my success.

> **If I could create more of a connection between my conscious and subconscious, I could supercharge my success.**

Those were the seeds of thought planted by a handful of books I read between airports. As my interest grew,

I discovered that many of the best books on the topic had already been classics for many years. Much of the commentary was traced to names like Andrew Carnegie, Charles Schwab, Thomas Edison, Woodrow Wilson, and numerous other superstars of achievement. Why hadn't I heard of this before?

Before long, I began to experiment with techniques for leveraging the untapped resources of my brain. Essentially, I was learning to create deliberate assignments for my subconscious – assignments that would lead to the accomplishment of various goals for my life. I wouldn't say I was 100% convinced, but I gave it enough credence to dive in and give it a shot.

The early results were so impressive, that I quickly realized my "normal" goals equated to under-achievement compared to my true potential. Instead of striving for top salesman in my region, I would need to set my sights on breaking records. My net earnings goals had to be revised from seven-figures to eight, and eventually to nine. Everywhere I applied these skills in life, the results seemed explosive.

> **My net earnings goals had to be revised from seven-figures to eight, and eventually to nine.**

Let me share some specific examples here. I'm not trying to be dramatic, but some of these still give me chills. So just to keep from sounding mystical, I'll also give you my best explanation for why these methods work.

When I first began to experiment with these concepts, I picked a set of goals. Everything I'd read said to be very specific, describing as many important details as possible. I bought a micro-cassette recorder to use for one of the recommended exercises. During my commute to work each morning, I would talk about my goals out loud in the car while the recorder captured my words. In vivid detail, I described life as I saw it once my goals were attained. I talked about my position in a new job in technical sales. I didn't know exactly where or what, but I audaciously depicted myself as the new number one salesman in the country. I described the emotions I felt winning a distinguished sales award, and I imagined what I might say when asked to address my peers at the annual sales meeting. I even declared what my paycheck would be when that day eventually arrived.

I didn't stop at career goals either. I also described the home my wife and I would purchase after moving to Orlando, FL, a strategic relocation that we had been discussing for some time. Virtually every aspect of life was painted with words like a verbal forecast of things to come. I saw myself driving a red Corvette, owning my own business, and even having my own airplane.

In those days, I was driving a pea-green Honda Accord that had been handed down to us from my wife's aunt. It had sheepskin seat covers and was such a bomb that if Homeland Security had existed back then, they would have confiscated it to protect American citizens. But for a few moments every day, I would drive along almost oblivious to my actual surroundings as I carried out this exercise of speaking life into the mental pictures that I called goals.

On the way home from work, I would rewind the tape and listen to what I had recorded on the way in that morning. This became my consistent routine. Every few weeks, I would fill up a tape, toss it in the glove box of that old green Honda Accord, and load a fresh tape.

I think everybody sees flashes of imaginary events they wish would come true. We've all imagined winning the lottery, being in a position of esteem, meeting that perfect someone, or hitting a buzzer-beater to win the championship. But this was different. I wasn't just wishing out loud for the things I was describing, I was declaring my intentions. I understood that I would have to work hard to earn my way toward them. And I didn't just sit by the front door waiting for Ed McMahon to drive up and give me a giant check that would change my life. I was actually working on strategies to start putting those dreams in motion.

> **I wasn't just wishing out loud for the things I was describing, I was declaring my intentions.**

To add to my routine of painting my subconscious with my goals and dreams I would stop by Denny's restaurant every morning at 7 AM to have coffee and set goals in each area of my life.

These were visions for how I wanted life to be if I could be the master painter of the canvas called my life. I kept them written on a stack of 4 x 6 note cards I carried with me, each one with a different goal on it. Day after day, I repeated this routine until my dreams were as familiar to my mind as reality itself.

Five years went by, and one day I was cleaning out the basement. I hadn't thought much about those days driving back and forth to work in that old pea-green Honda. The goals I'd had back then had evolved by now. Goals always do. As you achieve one milestone, you start to focus on the next, and so on. Eventually, we get so busy living in the present that daily details fade silently into the past. Such was the case with that first season of experimenting with the micro-cassette recorder.

But as I opened one particular box in the basement that day, I discovered a time machine that would connect my present to my past. The box was filled with the contents from that glove box in the old, green Honda. And it included a stack of micro-cassette tapes. Out of curiosity, I popped in one of the tapes and began to listen. As I lay there on the basement floor, I heard my own voice reaching out through that little speaker like the scratchy recording of an ancient prophet predicting the future. The old me had an alarming boldness as he attempted what was essentially a narration of the guy who was now lying on the floor listening. But even more alarming was the accuracy of his predictions.

The voice described the move to Orlando and my job in software sales, both of which had actually been a reality for nearly three years by then. He told of the #1 sales award and the speech, which had taken place just as he described, in front of a national sales force of 300 in Hawaii. To the guy on the tape, it was a visionary goal; to the guy listening, it was now a memory of one of the highlights of my career. It was such an uncanny mirroring of two worlds that I felt glad I had the plaque to help me keep them straight. About the only detail the guy on the tape left out was the actual name of the company where I accomplished it! And that's not all. Somehow, this cryptic futurist even knew that I now drove a red Corvette, and had my own business on the side. And when he guessed my salary with convincing accuracy, goose bumps covered my body.

> **There's natural power in our subconscious that we don't often leverage.**

Now, I'm not trying to suggest that there was supernatural power in those exercises, or that you can predict your future using micro-cassettes. But I am saying that there's natural power in our subconscious that we don't often leverage. And I don't think I could have accomplished so many specific goals at once without putting my subconscious to work to help work out all those details.

When the goose bumps went away, I analyzed the situation with a healthy measure of skepticism. After all, it's not hard to explain the red Corvette, the move to Orlando, or the job change. There's no magic in saving up for a certain car, applying for a certain job, or relocating to a new town. And there's probably no magic in starting your own company, or resolving to become the #1 guy on a national sales force. All I did was point at the outfield bleachers before hitting the home run. It gives the story a legendary air. But at the end of the day, it was just another home run.

And I think that's the whole point. There's no magic in the accomplishment of any of those goals. It's not like I'd grown a magic beanstalk, or laid a golden egg, or turned myself into a leprechaun.

Magic, no. But power, yes.

That experience got my attention. I couldn't help thinking that engaging my subconscious had made a night-and-day difference in the course of my life. It was like having three or four brains figuring out my life at once. Thinking back, it seemed fairly simple. Anybody will accomplish more if they get resolved and focused. All I did was choose deliberate goals and then focus more intently on achieving them.

With results like that, why wouldn't a person do that all the time?

I think the main reason we don't live like that is because we don't understand it. Even after living through it, I can't quite explain everything that goes on. People don't practice regularly what they can't explain practically. We just don't pursue things long-term unless there's a scientific promise of the outcome.

Lacking irrefutable science, the advocates of these concepts often focus on the "magic" of it. In the process, they end up sounding like they're selling foo-foo dust. And we're not buying it.

My experience tells me that you won't succeed if you think its magic. You can't. If you think it's magic then you'll just wish for it and wait for the magic to happen. In contrast, this has nothing to do with wishing and waiting. It requires organizing your thoughts, creating and revising strategies, and a willingness to work the plan. That's not magic at all.

The micro-cassette exercise was one of several tools I learned for reinforcing my goals. I also had goal cards that were like flash cards for each of my ambitions. I would keep them on the dashboard of my car and browse through them at red lights. Those objectives were so ingrained in my thoughts that the rest of me had almost no choice but to follow along. In any given situation, I felt myself evaluating my actions based on whether they supported my goals or not.

When faced with a purchase decision, or an opportunity, I gravitated naturally in the direction I intended to go, instead of wandering off course or giving in to an impulse. I don't mean to sound like there was no spontaneity in my life. It just wasn't the kind of spontaneity that would undermine the plan.

Needless to say, my success with those exercises has earned them a role in almost every season of life since. I've experimented with different techniques and stretched myself to varying degrees. But the basic idea hasn't changed much. And to be perfectly honest, my understanding of the principles hasn't deepened all that much either. Maybe it's not for us to understand exactly what goes on within the complexities of the human brain. All I know is that these things work.

> Maybe it's not for us to understand exactly what goes on within the complexities of the human brain. All I know is that these things work.

At one point my wife and I invited several friends to hold regular discussions about our goals, as well as our progress toward them. We met every couple of weeks for about six months and we shared our dreams and suggestions for taking the next step. To test some of my own theories, we held a contest to see who could spot the most red Jeep vehicles in one week. The cars were to be counted during normal drive times, and I gave everyone a card and a pen to keep in the car for scoring. The winner would get dinner on me at an expensive restaurant. The competition was fierce. In the course of a week, most people reported seeing a dozen or more qualifying vehicles. One man recorded 42 sightings.

It made for an interesting week. But the fascinating developments came after the contest was over. After working so intensely all week to find cars of that description, everyone had red Jeeps on the brain. And now they seemed to be popping up everywhere. Whether you looked for them or not. As a running joke for the next several weeks, people would "complain" about seeing so many, like a song that gets stuck in your head.

That little contest convinced all of us how the subconscious takes cues from our conscious thoughts and attempts to contribute to our progress. Like a day-glow highlighter, it scans the landscape and underlines the things we've said are important. It's so mechanical and methodical, that it doesn't even stop when the contest ends. And if it can help us spot cars on a crowded highway, maybe it can help us recognize opportunities when they come our way, or goals we dream of attaining. And that little bit of extra momentum could be just the factor we need to exploit them.

The findings and conversations from that first group led to other discussions with similar groups, and eventually to a resource called Blueprint for Life, a collection of numerous exercises and other thoughts on the subject. People have used Blueprint for Life, reported significant results, and recommended it to friends. Several notable companies have adopted it as a training tool, taking their employees through the process to enhance their performance at work. Now almost 20,000 people have experienced Blueprint for Life.

For my part, I was permanently changed. Reaching such grandiose goals so consistently sent me re-thinking my expectations and standards for success. Still in my twenties, I turned my thoughts to my ultimate achievement: total financial freedom. And with that bit of clarity at the young age of 30, I would soon find myself sitting by the pool with enough money to retire.

Chapter 5

BOREDOM AND FRUSTRATION BY THE POOLSIDE

So thanks to my secret weapon, I not only had the gumption to set the goal of becoming the number one salesman in the country, but I actually accomplished it. And that's not all. I think it's just as important that so many of my other goals were attained as well. In many respects, you could say that my life was everything I dreamed it could be... literally.

I think success like that could easily tempt someone to feel cocky and want to write a book about it so the whole world knows how well you're doing. But I want to emphasize that I don't see it that way at all. Maybe I picked it up as a result of growing up in Enterprise, Alabama, and being surrounded by people who hadn't lost perspective even though they rocketed from worst to first. From my vantage point, the principles hold the power, not me. I don't present myself as a sales genius or a self-made hero. If anything, I'm trying to impress on you the nature of these concepts to take a fairly ordinary guy like me and exploit every ounce of potential inside. I'm writing a book about it, but my real desire is not to tell you about me, but about these tools, in hopes that you'll begin to imagine an ultimate version of yourself emerging from your own dreams of what could be – whether you long to boost your career, or become more mature in some key relationships, or climb Mt. Everest, or achieve some humanitarian milestone with your life.

I'm moved by the potential for anyone to discover these principles and to move into overdrive with the things you consider important.

Along with the distinction of being the top salesman came the commissions from my sales. I was earning more than I ever imagined. Any income goals I'd set in the preceding months were long since overshadowed by the growing balance in my bank account. As a result, I suddenly found myself in a position to realize another one of my big goals: starting my own business.

Michele and I had always dreamed of owning a restaurant. She has a knack for taking a venue and giving it a sense of environment so things feel special. That includes concocting interesting treats or satisfying entrees that make a person feel like they're being taken care of. Of course, I was intrigued by the business potential of it. And I couldn't imagine a better scenario than working together with my wife. So with our own seed money and enthusiasm, we found a palm-lined street in Winter Park, FL and opened Nature's Table, featuring health-conscious original fare in a cozy setting.

I continued to work in sales while Michele handled most of the day-to-day restaurant duties. In light of the attention I was devoting to our new pet project, my productivity at work was nothing like it had been. As far as I was concerned, I was beginning a transition that would eventually take me out of the corporate world and into a full-time position in our family-run business.

At first it was very encouraging. People noticed the uniqueness of our menu and they commented on the atmosphere we created. Things were looking up. But the restaurant business can be challenging. The hazards are significant, while the upside is often less than proportionate to the risk. That's especially the case in the category of upscale quick-service that we had chosen to enter.

Over time, we encountered a wide variety of obstacles and setbacks. I give us credit for being flexible and responding with good solutions. However, I'll admit that most days felt like an uphill struggle.

To shorten a much longer story, the restaurant never lost the umbilical cord that connected it to our personal savings. Rather than wean and take on a life of its own, it slowly drained any extra income we'd saved from my success in sales. And what little attention it required from me was enough to ensure that I wouldn't be able to give my sales job the level of focus required to produce another huge windfall. There were enough positive signs in the restaurant to encourage us to keep trying. But in the end, those little victories just prolonged what turned out to be a slow death. I remember nights where I sat on the bed and crunched numbers trying to figure out how to pay the bills to keep the business open. And I recall being driven to tears over the realization that it was time to close up shop.

On the day we terminated our lease and sold off the restaurant's assets, we were left with about $20,000 to our name. It was a low point that rivaled my drive home from Florida to Enterprise as a teenager years earlier. To have all that money and lose it was something I'd never felt before. It was almost worse than never having it in the first place. Almost.

Fortunately, the experience of rising to the top had planted a seed of hope in me. I knew what it felt like to generate wealth, and I was convinced that I could do it again. Best of all, the setback of having to start all over again was actually the spark of motivation that launched me into what would prove to be my most lucrative line of work.

I had been interested in the stock market since college. And with the extra savings from my good run as a salesman, I finally had my first opportunity to try my hand at investing. So during the time that my primary attention was split between the restaurant and my other day job, I was dabbling as an investor.

> **It's funny how a person's calling in life has a way of finding its way to the surface, no matter what.**

It's funny how a person's calling in life has a way of finding its way to the surface, no matter what. I'd never sat down and decided to make a career of making money in the financial markets. I was never against it. But it never really crossed my mind to pursue it full time. On the other hand, there were plenty of other pursuits I'd thrown myself into. I'd gone after a career in engineering with tenacity. I gave some of my best years to earning an MBA so I could work in business. I worked ferociously to hone my effectiveness in sales. And I poured my heart and life savings into owning my own restaurant. In each case, great effort was expended. And every reward came at a high price. Nothing was easy.

Then along came my calling.

With minimal thought or intention, I'd wandered into something that would have more impact than ten lifetimes at any of my other ventures. That's the way it is when you discover your sweet spot. Everything flows naturally from deep inside your being. Your instincts guide you. And profit seems to come with minimal exertion. That was my early experience with investing.

Within two years, I'd managed to turn $20,000 into almost a million dollars.

Within two years, I'd managed to turn that $20,000 into almost a million dollars. I was able to spot pressure points in various markets and take up positions before the prices moved. I researched some emerging technologies and spread my risks in a way that would allow me to ride those waves without taking too many chances. It was a good economy too. And I probably had my share of luck. But I truly enjoyed the analytical side of investing. It was an outlet for my engineering interests I'd never known before.

The combination of success and enjoyment was enough to persuade me to think I'd reached the ultimate finish line for an executive. By all appearances, it looked like the money question had been permanently answered for me. If I could produce a 5,000% gain in a portfolio as a part-time investor, then managing my million or so as a full-time investor would provide more than I could earn in sales at any company. Not to mention, being a full-time investor was basically the same as having my own business. It seemed like the final destination for any executive career.

There's a basic understanding in American culture: you work until you can afford to live off your investments. And whenever your net worth is sufficient to carry you the rest of the way – or when you win the lottery – you quit your job, play golf, and watch the stock market. That's what I'd been told since grade school. And it's what the whole world seemed to be working toward. In fact, the earlier you can "retire", the more years you can spend playing golf and pursuing other extravagantly unimportant activities. The richer you are, the more extravagant and unimportant they can be.

> The earlier you can "retire", the more years you can spend playing golf and pursuing other extravagantly unimportant activities.

Of course, I was only thirty and still had another thirty or forty productive years left. But that didn't matter. The way I understood the game of life at the time, that just meant I was winning big time – like when your team is so far ahead at halftime that you pull all the starters and let the subs finish the game.

So at the age of thirty, I retired.

At first, it was like paradise. I'd spend a couple of hours each morning checking my investments and planning any trades that needed to be made. Then I'd hit the gym to lift weights before sitting by the pool for the afternoon. Every day, I followed basically the same routine – invest, exercise, sit; invest, exercise, sit.

After a few months of that lifestyle, I was starting to feel empty inside. I didn't think much about it. After all, I'd always pictured myself doing volunteer work for a campaign or helping at a non-profit during retirement. Apparently, my emptiness was the result of overlooking this unmet goal. Therefore, my solution was to round out my tidy routine by getting involved in a few causes that were meaningful.

The change helped. But it wasn't enough. My finances were good, my lifestyle was like a vacation, I was happy in marriage, and my mind was occupied with worthwhile causes. As a person of faith, I was even active in my church. I was doing everything a person could do to experience satisfaction and fulfillment. And yet, it eluded me. I was restless, like a racehorse that just can't wait for the gates to fling open. I longed to run, but there was no track in sight.

Eventually I would come to realize that for me, life was more about being in the race than crossing the finish line. I was born to work and create – to produce something. At that stage of life, I wasn't ready to stand around in the winner's circle with flowers around my neck. I was itching to go all out. Not only that, I really yearned to be working in my sweet spot, applying myself in the investment world that seemed to suit me so well. Without that component in my life, I could never be completely happy.

My experience was so different from what I'd expected. Everything I'd read or heard up to that point had focused on the goal of making money. Everyone around me – including my coworkers and leaders in business – had led me to think that crossing the financial finish line was what it's all about. Somehow, all my training and goal-setting revolved around becoming so good at what I did that I wouldn't have to do it anymore.

In my haste to live up to my potential, I never stopped to question my understanding of the race I was running. I assumed it was a sprint to the finish. But now I was starting to get a different picture. Maybe it wasn't so much about finishing at all. Maybe it was more about pacing yourself in such a way that you actually enjoy the experience itself. Imagine that.

Come to think of it, it's like anything. If it's worth doing, then it's worth enjoying. Presumably, your career should be something worth doing, not something you hate so much you can't wait for it to be over. I mean, it's great to have the finances to choose between the two. But just having the money isn't enough. It doesn't make you satisfied. Playing golf all day, or sitting by the pool doesn't do it either. At least not for long. Work is a natural part of life. And if you take it out too early, it's like a key part of life is gone. True fulfillment in life comes from doing what you were created to do – to pursue a calling.

> **True fulfillment in life comes from doing what you were created to do – to pursue a calling.**

It had nothing to do with money after all.

As a person of faith, I'd always known that being fulfilled had something to do with having my heart connected to my Creator. But as I was finding out, that was only half the picture. The other half was just plain practical. In spiritual terms, my heart also had to be connected to the thing for which I was created. Somehow, there was a mission in the simple task of working. Every day, there was a purpose for being alive. And I would only feel alive if I lived each day on purpose.

It reminds me of Eric Liddel, the runner in Chariots of Fire. He said, "When I run, I feel God's pleasure." Maybe I'd retire someday. But in the meantime, there was still some running to do. And as much as I enjoy sitting by the pool, there was no pleasure like running my appointed race each day.

So back out of retirement I came.

I was committed to a career in investments now. And since I'd already achieved the goal of becoming a millionaire, un-retirement would require setting goals that would stretch me even further. Logically, I would need to think in terms of tens of millions, instead of millions. Instead of just my own portfolio, I started thinking of ways to apply my skills in broader arenas. I began to manage money for other people as well. Based on my success to date, I was entrusted with investing money for a handful of other individuals. I continued to do well, and more investors came on board.

At that point, I decided to move my operation out of our house and into an office. Since it was just me, it seemed odd to rent a space by myself, so I was interested in sharing something with a compatible office mate. A friend of mine named Eric Swartz was also looking to defray expenses. He was an institutional broker, which sounded complementary to my line of work. So we began co-renting together.

The arrangement was working quite well. I pretty much kept to myself, and he kept to himself. Occasionally we'd borrow pens or printers, or check each other's mailbox. Our paths would cross, but our careers remained separate, parallel endeavors.

But one day, I got a strange call from Eric. He sounded distressed and frustrated. He had never been a man of many words, but now he was almost speechless. When he reached me, I was at a meeting out of town. "You've got to get back here," he said. I pressed him to find out what was going on. "You have to help me with this," was all he blurted. Somehow, I got just enough fragmented information out of him to discern that he was over his head in a major project. I didn't know what he had in mind. And I was sure he didn't quite either. But I headed back home to see what I could do.

Little did I know that a partnership was about to be born.

And hundreds of millions were about to be made.

Chapter 6

WHAT GOES UP

If it hadn't been for our humble beginnings, I might never have ended up paired with Eric, nor would we have discovered such an incredible niche in an extremely profitable business. The space we shared was inside a 70s-era two-story promenade awkwardly situated between a Dunkin Donuts and a Hooter's Restaurant.

The inside wasn't any better.

At a meager $400 per month, we were getting about what we paid for it. The layout was a basic square no larger than 30 by 30. It was divided into three little workspaces, a hallway entrance, and a simple bathroom long overdue for renovation. The old toilet was weak and deliberate, taking almost a full minute to complete a flush. Its close proximity to the phones meant that conference calls had to be carefully scheduled so as to avoid times when the plumbing was likely to be active.

Although we ran separate businesses at first, Eric and I were destined to become familiar with each other's work, thanks largely to our compressed office configuration and its college dorm overtones. Each of us also employed an assistant, so there were actually four of us crammed into that little space. As a result, we were practically piled on top of each other as we worked. There's an old adage about a shoeshine boy who learned to be a stockbroker just by listening to the conversation of his customers. And after working in that little office, I'm a believer in such stories. Without even trying, we knew the ins and outs of each other's schedules, clients, and annoying habits.

So when Eric suggested the idea of working together, it wasn't my first exposure to his business concept. After his frantic call for help, I returned to Atlanta to discuss it.

Eric, is a visionary. Translation: he thinks up things to do faster than anyone can do them. Including himself. In fact, most visionaries don't even know how to pull off their own ideas. So they need other people around them to round out the team. That's how Eric and I came together.

Being a visionary is a lot like being the conductor of an orchestra. The conductor looks at a symphony or a concerto on paper and he starts to imagine how the violas and the cellos will establish a soft voice of harmony while the first violins lay their delicate melody on top like the final coat of wax on a rare, collectible car. If everything goes as he envisions, the performance will be magical.

But the conductor can't play all those instruments himself. In most cases, he can't play any of them as well as the virtuosos assembled before him. And that can either be the most satisfying or the most frustrating thing in the world. If one or two violinists can't quite get it right, or if a cello misses a downbeat, the conductor feels like a carpenter with a dull saw. He can't fulfill his vision. It's aggravating.

When Eric called me that day, he was like a conductor without an orchestra. He had a strong business plan that involved connecting private equity investors with emerging small-cap companies. But like a lot of visionaries, Eric had an idea that was bigger than he was. He had written a beautiful symphony, but there was no way he could play all the instruments by himself. What he needed was someone with an analytical mind who could design the systems necessary to support the operation. He needed someone familiar with financial markets. And some experience in sales wouldn't hurt either.

We'd started out with a random notion to share office space and ended up being the perfect complements to each other's skill set. Within a few minutes of our discussion, the pieces were falling into place. Remember, I was an engineer. So even with my eyes closed, I could see what was needed to round out Eric's utterly brilliant business opportunity. I saw how Eric could shake the trees with the CEOs of companies looking for capital, and I could begin building the syndicate of investors. In addition, I would shore up the legal documents and analyst reports to spell out the details of the investment offerings.

It was the middle of the 1990s. The economy was growing like never before. And that bullish growth left a lot of established companies in need of capital to expand, to restructure, or to enter new markets. Even healthy companies could have a hard time generating enough cash to keep up with the expansion needed to exploit the opportunities. The solution? Private equity – high-yield investments from institutional investors outside of the public exchanges.

In those days, the recipe for success was simple: take a good idea and back it with enough capital to put it on the map. Once the stock garnered enough momentum to catch the eye of bigger investors, it was often swept along to even higher heights. As a result, early adopters were rewarded for being first on board with these rising companies. Private equity meant huge returns for many investors. And companies couldn't prime the market pump without capital from these private investors. They needed each other.

Together, Eric and I were perfectly positioned to serve both sets of needs.

The company was called Swartz Investments. It was basically a placement agency, or match-making service, between Institutional Investors and the companies so anxious to find this type of capital. We built relationships with investors who were looking for such opportunities, and we kept a database of companies who were seeking new rounds of funding. Wherever their interests overlapped, we brought them together.

The secret engine behind Eric's business concept was the invention of a new type of security we created and developed called a Variable Rate Debenture. We didn't know it at the time, but we were actually pioneering a new category in the financial industry, one that accounts for billions annually today. Once the word got out, competition would be fierce. But in the meantime, we were flying solo and under the radar. The whole pie was ours for the taking.

The impetus for Eric's plea for help was the angst he felt trying to coordinate the details of his first deal. So the good news is that he already had a lead on the first customer when I walked in the door. Now we just had to figure out how to put it all together.

After an initial scramble, I managed to organize the prerequisite paperwork to move forward. Once we were officially hired to raise money for our first customer, it was mostly a matter of formalizing the verbal agreements

> **We didn't know it at the time, but we were pioneering a new category in the financial industry that accounts for billions annually today.**

we'd laid out with some investors before the fact. When the deal finally closed, it was pretty reassuring. It showed that our plan actually worked. In it, we raised $1.2 million for a pharmaceutical company. Just like that, we brought in $100,000 for our effort.

That was a big moment for me. Although I was already managing my own portfolio – and had been in and out of "retirement" – I was far from financially independent. I still drove a minivan, paid a mortgage, and needed to make money. Of course, by the time we paid our assistants' salaries and the rent, there was nothing left for me from that first commission. But it proved that our model worked. And I was encouraged.

The next deal came shortly after. And it was similar in size. Now I could start to imagine how I might actually draw a nice salary from this venture.

And then came the third deal.

The third deal involved a technology company that would enable companies to take all their documents and scan them to a digital database. That was big news back in the 1990s. And the company was seeking about five times more than our two previous projects. This one had real promise.

Based on our growing momentum, the all-important investor base was starting to grow. We would need every bit of it to raise the $5 million we'd been charged to find for this company. Our approach involved offering commissions to freelance "finders" for bringing qualified investors to the table. Because of this technique, our network expanded around the world almost overnight as our finders brought great investors to us from all corners of the world. Eric and I were coming to work in the wee hours of the morning to manage calls between European investors and the ones in the states. Remember, at this time in the economy, finding investor capital was almost synonymous with closing the deal. And when it came to finding money, we'd hit the jackpot. Among the sources we courted were several large European banks and the Saudi Arabian royal family.

Within a short time of signing the documents to begin raising funds for the document scanning company, the offers for this exciting new business started rolling in. We raised one million... then two.... Before long we reached the goal $5 million. So we called the company and told them the great news. In light of the demand for their stock, we asked if they were interested in extending the offer beyond the $5 million mark. They didn't mind the idea of extra cash, so they doubled the deal to $10 million. And in the process, they doubled the potential earnings Eric and I would gross from the deal.

We hit the streets again and continued to find receptive investors. When we reached $10 million, we called again and asked if they wanted us to stop. This time they raised the target to $15 million. And when we went back to the market, the cycle began to repeat itself. Finally, the CEO of the company instructed us to raise just as much as we could raise.

When the dust settled, we had put together roughly $23 million for the document scanning company. And that resulted in about $1.5 million in fees for us. Just like that we'd made over a million dollars from the proceeds of our business together.

Yes, I was starting to think this must be what "rich" feels like.

In the months that followed, the deals continued to roll in. One deal a month. Two deals a month. The money kept rolling in. From all over the world, investors began to seek us out to get in on the deals we were putting together. It was a feeding frenzy.

> **We'd made over a million dollars from the proceeds of our business together. Yes, I was starting to think this must be what "rich" feels like.**

To service all this business, we began to hire analysts and managers. All this growth came so quickly that we were still crammed into the same space next to that Dunkin Donuts. We couldn't find a bigger office fast enough. At one point there were a dozen or so people jammed in there together. Needless to say, while we were brokering multi-million-dollar transactions between companies and investors, we were testing the structural integrity of that little office space. As you might imagine, by the time everybody finished their first cup of coffee, people were lined up like the jets at the Atlanta airport during Christmas holidays, waiting their turn to punish that poor old toilet. In a situation like that, I'm not sure which is worse: suffocation by air freshener, or suffocation without it.

Eventually we found a larger office.

> **In our first three years together, we placed enough capital to generate $50 million in commissions and fees for our firm.**

In our first three years together, we placed enough capital to generate $50 million in commissions and fees for our firm. By our fourth year, we'd put together more than half a billion (yes, with a B!) in placements and were employing about 35 analysts, investment bankers, and attorneys to keep track of our growing list of transactions.

In addition to fees from placements, we also negotiated warrants against the shares we issued. So as those stocks continued to grow in the months that followed, we found ourselves amassing a portfolio worth even more than the income from brokering the original transactions.

If you'd told me this story about myself as a kid, I might have picked this point as the moment when I walk off into the sunset and live happily ever after. I'd already earned more money than my small town dreams could contain. Forget what I thought "rich" was before. This must be it.

But as it turned out, the Variable Rate Debenture was just a warm-up.

There's an old saying that goes, "Money begets money." And to some degree, that became the case for us. The success we had as a placement agency opened the door for our next great opportunity. What made us unique was our almost strange combination of skills and ambitions. At the heart of it, we were entrepreneurs and inventors. We were driven by the idea of doing something that hadn't been done before. With my engineering background, I could have just as easily ended up developing new kinds of aircraft, or weapons for the Defense Department. But we were in finance. And in a way, we were there to invent new forms of money.

The notion of creating new types of securities was fascinating. Where most investment professionals carve out market share with existing tools, we felt like we had been granted the freedom to invent new tools and thereby discover new worlds in finance. It's probably not unlike the way the explorers of Christopher Columbus' day felt. Back then, it was one thing to work the existing trade routes; but the idea of discovering a short cut to India was always looming in the back of their minds. And to think there was a whole, new continent teeming with resources just waiting to be discovered – well, that was a game-changer.

By now we had experience working with the SEC. We knew the ropes of registering new products and fulfilling the various legal requirements. So I think it was our natural inclination to imagine what we could invent next as an encore.

The idea of a virtual ATM that took draws against corporate equity wasn't completely new. It had been around in various forms for some time. Our version of the concept was a security structure we called a Private Equity Line, and it was actually a special type of security that we designed and registered with the SEC. Technically, it worked like a continuous stock offering, allowing an investor to purchase shares of stock as the company needed infusions.

The beautiful thing about the Equity Line was that the timing was so perfect. It was now 1998, and the dot-com phenomenon was just revving up. The Equity Line was the perfect new mousetrap, giving all the new startup technology companies exactly what they wanted and needed: access to cash.

Also in that year, we launched a proprietary fund that exclusively offered – you guessed it – Equity Line Financings to small, public companies. In three short years, between 1998 and 2001, we closed 54 Equity Line transactions.

My definition of rich was changing almost daily.

Growing up, there were the usual shifts in what I thought it looked like to be rich. But I certainly expected to land on a general definition by the time I settled into a career. I guess I assumed that everybody who wore a suit, drove a new car, and owned a nice home was considered to be in a general category called "rich". But the further I got, it seemed there were more and more degrees and flavors of rich than ever. Instead of crossing a finish line, the road just kept going. Every mountain I crested only brought the next highest peak into view. Was there any end to it all?

Week in and week out, we collected impressive fees. But even more significant was the increasing value of our portfolio of options. The higher the market climbed, the more ridiculous its value got.

Our portfolio grew to $50 million in value, then $100 million, then over $200 million.

Meanwhile, we quickly outgrew our new office space despite having already knocked out a wall to double it. We'd come a long way from the oversized bathroom beside the Dunkin Donuts. But where we were headed, we were going to need an executive headquarters to rival the world's top financial institutions.

> **Our private portfolio grew to $50 million in value, then $100 million, then over $200 million.**

If I was having trouble fathoming the numbers on our financial statement, then one look at this new office should provide a picture of what big-time wealth looks like. I've visited the offices of some of the biggest names in the industry. And ours remains the nicest I've ever seen to this day. It offered the perfect combination of panache and functionality we needed to recruit CEO clients and entertain fund managers and other investor partners. We had the entire penthouse floor to ourselves. The place was loaded with travertine marble and wood grain. The paneled boardroom had all the latest electronic gadgets for high-end multimedia presentations. And in the middle of it all, we built an authentic 50's diner – complete with chrome soda stools, checkerboard tile, and booths with coin-operated jukeboxes. The whole thing was run by "Miss Vicky", who doubled as concierge and short-order chef. No expense was spared to give employees and visitors the ultimate environment for achieving success as a world-wide financial player.

Now that you mention it, the definition of rich wouldn't be complete without an office like the one we built. And so my ever-sprawling picture evolved again.

Then came my fortieth birthday. That's when I experienced a moment so surreal I still can't help wondering if it was just a dream. Michele and I had rented a 110 foot yacht to mark my fourth decade.

With a cool drink in one hand and shrimp cocktail in the other, I casually closed a deal that earned us $1.5 million that day.

We were sailing from Martha's Vineyard up to Nantucket and Newport. While lounging on the deck of the boat one afternoon, I got a call on my cell phone from a client who wanted to make a draw from the fund. It wasn't the largest transaction we'd ever done. But it certainly wasn't small. So with a cool drink in one hand and shrimp cocktail in the other, I casually closed a deal that earned us $1.5 million that day. I'll admit, it felt like a scene from a movie.

Okay, let's be honest. The richest man on the planet couldn't top a moment like that. Even if I were to amass more money some day, I'd just had the ultimate "rich" experience. Certainly I could close the book on my understanding of the concept.

This was definitely rich.

But as I would soon find out, not the kind of rich that lasts forever.

Chapter 7

Must Come Down

One of my favorite things about the investment business is traveling to the world centers where the banks are headquartered. Several of us in the company have made the rounds in Europe, Chicago, and New York for meetings. It's important to put feet on the street from time to time. And most of us savor the experience of being in the middle of the financial fray.

As a result, several of our employees were regulars in New York's financial district. Chuck and Glenn, two of our company's most trusted long-time managers, were often called on to make the trek to Manhattan to be our eyes and ears on the ground. Such was the case during this heyday of ultimate "rich" I've described.

It was September, and the freshness of a new season was in the

> **And today, they were scheduled to visit the epicenter of activity – the World Trade Center Towers.**

air. Back in Atlanta on this particular day, I stopped by the gym on the way to work. Pondering the day ahead of me, I was looking forward to getting a report from the field. Chuck and Glenn were right in the middle of several days of meetings in New York City. And today, they were scheduled to visit the epicenter of activity – the World Trade Center Towers.

When I walked through the doors with my gym bag in hand, the first thing I noticed was the long row of televisions above the exercise machines. They usually displayed a variety of options to suit everyone's diverse interests. But this time, the pictures all seemed strangely similar to one another. It was like they were all tuned in to the same thing from different camera angles. They all featured some form of graphic for a news flash. A plane had hit the World Trade Center.

Like many people, it didn't register at first. Your first thought is that it was an isolated accident, probably involving a small private plane and a handful of building occupants. Upon seeing the extent of damage, you wonder if it might actually involve a commercial plane. When the second plane hit, the picture suddenly came into focus. Eventually I learned about the crash at the Pentagon and the multiple hijackings taking place simultaneously across the country.

Then it hit me. Chuck and Glennn are in those buildings today!

We are not a large company. The most we employed at our height was about 50 people. We were like extended family to each other. Chuck and Glenn were the guys who shared the emotional twists and turns of a growing business with each other. They were your audience for trying out a new joke. They brought meals for your family when you had a baby. That's just the kind of bond we shared. And Chuck and Glenn had been there almost from the beginning. Oftentimes, it was Chuck and Glenn who came in early to scour the market reports in order to report the good or bad news when the rest of us arrived for the day.

Frantically, I started dialing my cell phone.

Despite several attempts, I couldn't get either of them on the phone. I fought back the mental images that might explain why they didn't respond. Next I called the office to see if anyone had heard from them. No one had. Awkwardly, we called their wives – first Jill, then Amanda. They described a similar predicament. So the waiting began.

An hour went by.

Then two.

The wait was excruciating.

At last, the phone rang. Chuck's wife had finally gotten word from them. As it turned out, they were among the millions of New Yorkers who evacuated on foot. Call it fate or Providence, but their meetings in the Towers were scheduled for that afternoon. And as it turned out, the terrorists had scheduled their attacks for the morning.

A mere sliver of time – a few hours – turned out to be the difference between walking away unharmed and being counted among the many lives lost that day.

Chuck and Glennn had to walk several miles to reach the ferry to New Jersey. About half the people on the boat with them were covered in white dust. No one spoke. As they disembarked, two lines formed. The dust-covered passengers were funneled into a line where they were required to be hosed down in case the powder contained some type of poisonous agent. The rest could depart normally.

Air travel was shut down. Many of the trains were either out of service or over-sold. And cabs were few and far between. Almost empty-handed, our two colleagues made their way to the home of a college friend a few hours away to spend the night. From there, they began scavenging from the remaining modes of transportation that were still in service. Almost three days later, they finally made it home.

We had escaped 9/11 much better than many. But the disaster wasn't finished with us yet. The economic events it triggered would reach us in waves throughout the weeks and months to come. The fall of the towers would turn out to be an omen of the financial devastation we would face.

> The fall of the towers would turn out to be an omen of the financial devastation we would face.

At its peak, our firm's proprietary portfolio reached about $200 million in market value. I can say it was the peak now; of course, at the time, it looked like the middle of the usual ups and downs along the way to long-term growth. To tell the story in hindsight, it's easy to assess what should have happened. When something reaches a peak, it's time to sell. But back then, of course, we had no way of knowing if the market was collecting itself for another big run or if it was about to decline. The whole experience of watching your portfolio rise that much is like being the frog in the kettle. The rise is so gradual that it's easy to lose touch with major milestones like the boiling point. Unless you pick your landmarks ahead of time, you'll glide right past them without noticing it. That's especially true with investments.

As you might have guessed by now, that peak was followed by a major correction. Rather, we wished it had been a correction. In reality, it was a severe decline. By the time the dust settled, our $200 million portfolio was hovering just below $20 million. Now, to the average person, $20 million is still plenty to do the things you want to do in life. And it's plenty for me too. But all I knew was we'd just lost $180 million. And that's a bad run no matter who you are.

> We'd just lost $180 million. And that's a bad run no matter who you are.

Our business model thrived on market liquidity. And to a similar degree, it suffered when the economy dried up. Just to put things in perspective, the NASDAQ 100 index lost roughly 80% of its value during that period. And the other markets weren't doing much better. Needless to say, people weren't interested in the emerging, small-cap securities we'd built our business around.

Our overhead at the time was in the neighborhood of $250,000 a month. So it wasn't long before we realized we had to scale back.

Slowly, we took up the miserable assignment of laying-off staff. First one. Then two. Then a handful. We tried to minimize the casualties in the hopes that things might turn around. Weeks would pass while everyone nervously awaited signs of hope. Somehow, all these meetings to let people go were held in the same red conference room. It became notorious for it. At one point it felt more like an execution chamber than a space designed for inking big deals. Rather than wait for the ax, several people left in search of solid ground. When all was said and done, almost 70% of our employees were gone.

The defining moment for me came when we were finally forced to abandon our beautiful penthouse office. It seemed like just a few weeks earlier I'd been lounging on a yacht, landing million-dollar commissions on my cell phone. And now I was driving a rented moving truck loaded with furniture back to a tiny office near the Dunkin Donuts where it all began.

> **Losing 90% of my wealth in one run was a painful reminder of just how quickly it can vanish.**

Yes, I liked being rich. But this kind of rich had some rough edges to it. It definitely wasn't the kind that would last forever. Losing 90% of my wealth in one run was a painful reminder of just how quickly it can vanish. Not only that, but having been to the top, I'd gotten a glimpse of money's inability to deliver complete happiness. It didn't hurt. But when I'm honest, the things that determined whether I was happy during that time had almost nothing to do with finances. I was starting to see that it wasn't the kind of rich you want to build your whole life around.

What strikes me most about that experience is not our failure to pick the right exit price for the stocks in our portfolio. What strikes me is my own failure to commit to a personal finish line for my financial life. At that point in my life, I had strategic goals for virtually anything that was important to me. In each case, my goals were designed to support some key aspect of my life – a financial need, an important relationship, or the pursuit of health. In that sense, my goals were always in touch with reality. They served a purpose.

But when it came to growing my net worth into the hundreds of millions, that wasn't the case. Sure, I wanted the growth. And I pursued it. But I didn't really have a reason for it. And that little lapse of intentionality opened the door to a big disappointment for me.

Remember, even as a teenager in Florida, I had my eyes set on the distant goal of exploring the world outside my hometown of Enterprise, Alabama. As a result, the biggest setback in my life at the time was a mere bump in the road that provided valuable information for the future. But now, at the age of forty and at the peak of success, I didn't have my eyes fixed on a value that extended beyond the success or failure of the moment. So I had nothing to show for everything I lost.

For the sake of example, what if I had been specific about some of the things I wanted to acquire in life. Suppose I had the written goal of owning a vacation home in Colorado, or my own jet airplane, or starting a special school for orphans in the inner city. With that level of clarity, I could have seized the opportunity to accomplish those things when the funds allowed. But without that kind of intentionality, I just kind of drifted along as my portfolio rose to the top, then plummeted back down again. At least I could have given the money to charity. What an incredible impact it would have had! I love "investing" in entrepreneurial non-profits. Imagine the difference it would have made to drop a couple million dollars or more into a handful of organizations like that. Such a move would barely have put a dent in my account. And the impact would have lived on far beyond the ups and downs of the market. But I didn't do that. And now the money was just gone – a missed set of unbelievable opportunities.

Throughout my professional life, I'd always had goals for moving to the next rung of the ladder. But somehow it had never occurred to me to include goals for what to do if I reached the top of the ladder. I say top because I think I'd pretty much accomplished my financial goals by that point. It's not something I decided consciously, but I sort of knew inside that I'd accumulated as much as I'd ever need or want. My wildest dreams for myself never required more than five or ten million dollars. So once the numbers got higher than that, I was in uncharted territory as far as having goals was concerned. In contrast, if I had dreamed of owning an airline or a professional sports team, I would have remained naturally strategic with every penny.

> It's a strange dilemma when your dreams don't keep pace with your opportunities.

It's a strange dilemma when your dreams don't keep pace with your opportunities. But that's what happened to me. And I don't think it's that uncommon. In fact, most people are sitting on more potential than they realize. More often than not, we simply lack the goals that would leverage the resources available to us. And any time that happens, we expose ourselves to that sinking feeling of lost opportunity.

Okay, so maybe you'd say you could live with $20 million instead of $200 million. But don't miss the point. No matter how big your bank account gets, you're still vulnerable to the disappointment and frustration and regret of missed opportunities. So it benefits anyone to consider this idea. Your goals need to stay in balance with your opportunities and accomplishments. Even if you never aspired to them in the first place. Wherever you find yourself rich beyond your dreams – whether it's wealth or an unexpected promotion or a relationship or just extra time on your hands – you'd be wise to rethink your goals with those things in mind. Dream a little. What hidden ambitions might be awakened, giving you satisfaction in the next chapter of your life? Is there anything undiscovered there? Or have you truly reached the point in your life where anything more is just extra? Develop goals around those things. If nothing else, set goals for their disposition. If it's extra money, decide how to give it away. If it's a position in a company, plan your exit. If it's extra time, think about the best ways to spend it. The point is this: even your "extra" can bring regret if you don't have goals for it.

By nature, we're very thoughtful about resolving the deficits in our lives. But we're not as good about resolving our abundances. When we need money for retirement, we start a savings plan. When we want a robust career, we pursue an education and build a strategic resume. But in those rare seasons when we find ourselves with extra wealth in those categories, we're not as good at managing the situation. In my experience, you can't overlook those without leaving the door open to the possibility of huge regret.

In my case, I made the mistake of thinking my financial retirement goal is a variable. I thought it was a moving target that I could simply raise whenever my portfolio grew. But it's not. If I plan properly, I should know my dollar goal right down to the penny. It should be a fixed number. Granted, if you give somebody a reasonable amount, they can figure out how to make ends meet. But we're talking about goals here.

It may seem like I'm splitting hairs, but let me explain. You see, I never pinpointed my retirement number specifically, but it was there in my gut all along. Somehow, I knew that I would never need more than about $10 million for myself and my family. That's just all I could ever need to fulfill every aspect of my purpose in life. Anything more would just spill out of my cup. I knew this about myself even though I never articulated it. Therefore, when my resources exceeded that amount, I misinterpreted the situation. Instead of recognizing the overage and planning the best possible action, I became unsure of my goals and began to entertain other ideologies that had no connection to me personally. By failing to define myself clearly, in the context of possessing $200 million, I missed my opportunity to decide what I would do if given that amount of "extra" wealth.

> **We assume that when the money overflows, happiness overflows with it.**

That's what can happen when your goals don't keep pace with your opportunities. In America, we don't typically see that one coming. Instead, we kind of like the idea of someday having more than we know what to do with. That's the ultimate portrayal of success in the movies. It's how they paint the celebrities and business moguls. We assume that when the money overflows, happiness overflows with it. But if that were true, why are there so many unhappy celebrities? I'm here to suggest that happiness is not addressed by abundance. Nor is it necessarily diminished by a deficit. Instead, it's more often determined by how well we manage the balance between our goals and our opportunities.

If you picture yourself retiring some day, you need to consider this idea. Because one day, you just might accumulate enough money to do so. And when you reach that point, you'll either recognize it because you've written the number down somewhere, or you just might cruise right past it thinking it's a variable thing. If you do the latter, you might soon find yourself wrestling with uncertainty regarding your purpose in life. In the worst case scenario, you can find yourself rich and miserable, like a tabloid celebrity.

> **In the worst case scenario, you can find yourself rich and miserable, like a tabloid celebrity.**

At some point, enough is enough. There's a limit to the millions an individual needs to accumulate in his lifetime. Somewhere out there, everybody has a limit. We don't usually think of it that way. If we reach a new level, we automatically look ahead to the next higher one as if anything else would be putting a limit on our potential. But that's the wrong notion. And it's not realistic. If we don't set goals within the context of reality – including how much is enough – then we set ourselves up for disappointment.

The whole experience of gaining and losing hundreds of millions led me to make some changes. I felt no need to watch idly while that level of wealth accumulated again. My regrets had nothing to do with the need for that kind of money anyway. The only thing I regretted was not doing the right thing with that kind of money when I had it.

So to prevent a similar situation, I decided on a financial finish line once and for all. It doesn't mean I can't change that number at some point in the future. But for now, I've set a maximum number on what I'll keep for myself. In my case, I was just being honest about the number that had been my gut feeling all along anyway.

The next question is what happens if I pass that amount again. After thinking through my goals, I've decided to get behind a handful of charities whose missions I value. Whenever my net worth rises above that waterline, I move the excess into a foundation that supports those charities.

Like I said before, at *least* that money could have gone to charity. But after thinking it through, that's actually the *most* I could have done too. Sure, I could think up new toys to give myself, or new vacation homes. However, it's possible to lose those too. But I could never lose the feeling of knowing I'd made a difference through those charities. If you ever wondered what can satisfy the man who has everything, I'd say this is it. Money doesn't really have any value unless it's used as a tool to do something of value. It's only as good as how you spend it. Spending it on

> **Money doesn't really have any value unless it's used as a tool to do something of value.**

yourself has its place. But for me, that's only one piece of the puzzle. In order to maximize monetary value, you must manage everything in a way that reflects your personal values. And that requires setting some goals to identify those values in the first place.

Money is a tool for happiness, not a source of it. I'm not ready to accept outright the old mantra that money can't buy happiness. I think money can actually have a role in the process. But only if you spend it right.

The events of 9/11 triggered a lot of soul-searching throughout the country. As the fragile nature of life played out on live television, we were brought collectively back to the realization that there's more to life than earning and spending. The terrorists managed to rock the American economy. But in the process they did us the unintended service of recalibrating the personal economy of everyone they impacted. As we were all reminded, world trade is only one element in the complex makeup of one's personal economy. If our grip on the financial piece was a bit too tight before, then loosening it freed our hands to lay hold again of that which really mattered to us all along.

How can money hold so much value and yet be so incapable of bringing satisfaction in certain situations? How is it such a key to happiness while constantly falling short of actually delivering it? I wanted to be rich forever. But several times now I had witnessed the shortcomings of money. Somehow, right at the point of ultimate payoff, money always seemed to lose its value.

I knew what life was like without money. And I knew what it was like with it. I'm not one to conclude that money has nothing to do with happiness, or that swearing off all materialism is required. I

> **Maybe there was a key ingredient I'd overlooked – a catalyst or an enhancer that would cure money's glaring inability to close the deal.**

just knew that there was something missing. Maybe money was only part of the recipe for "rich". Maybe there was a key ingredient I'd overlooked – a catalyst or an enhancer that would cure money's glaring inability to close the deal.

Or perhaps money isn't synonymous with rich after all. We think of them interchangeably. But maybe their relationship is more indirect.

A dollar bill is just a piece of paper. It's a proxy for the gold in a vault somewhere. What if money has a similar relationship to "rich"? What if money is just a representative of the thing that holds real value?

In that case, it would be worth any price to discover what it was. Especially when you consider that my net worth would soon soar above $100 million again.

Chapter 8

HOLISTIC RICHES

At the beginning of this book, I suggested that there are three types of "rich". And while money plays a role in all three, it does not define "rich" by itself. Money can be a tool to make you rich. But ultimately, "rich" is a much bigger concept than the balance of your bank account. Money plays a part. But it's really just a means to an end. In fact, money is a pretty poor measure of rich. Which is precisely why a person can have lots of money and still be miserable. Conversely, someone can have little in the way of financial resources but can be immensely wealthy.

All this brings us to the second dimension of rich we mentioned earlier. Remember, we said the first type refers to financial riches. But the second type is something I call "holistic" riches. And you can't be rich forever if you ignore this idea.

> **Money can be a tool to make you rich. But ultimately, "rich" is a much bigger concept than the balance of your bank account.**

As I stated before, even as a young boy I had many of the things we all want deep down inside. Family, friends, community, and a sense of purpose are examples I brought up in Chapter One. There are many different ways you could categorize these non-monetary aspects of rich. But the main point is that they exist. Like the famous MasterCard commercials point out, "There are some things money can't buy." And indeed, these are often priceless.

In order to be sure we're truly rich, we need a definition that not only counts money, but also measures how we're doing in all these other areas. As I look across the various aspects of life, I see five important categories that determine a person's sense of "rich". I call these categories "The Big 5". They are: Financial, Relationships, Career, Physical, and Spiritual. These are the five categories I monitor to ensure that in addition to financial riches, I'm not neglecting the holistic, "some-things-money-can't-buy" aspect of rich.

FINANCIAL

I don't need to say much about this one here. I've already lobbied you that financial goals are a vital – although incomplete – component of "rich". Everybody needs a financial plan. And this category represents that plan. If you already have a strategy for your monetary wealth, however, don't be too quick to drop it in place here. Once you ponder the other four categories, you might want to make some adjustments to your financial goals. You might decide you'll need more money to accomplish those other things. Or you might decide it's better to earn less money if it allows you to become richer in some of the other categories. Being rich across the board often requires some give-and-take in certain areas. And sometimes it's best to settle for less money if it allows you greater gains elsewhere.

RELATIONSHIPS

If I was happy growing up without much money, then where did that happiness come from? Whatever it was, clearly it would have to be an important part of the recipe for being rich forever. Growing up, I was rich because of all the relationships – family and friends – that were all around me. Happiness is not so much a matter of your lifestyle and possessions as it is the people with whom you share those things. In fact, I believe that relationships are the main event in life. Everything else – your career, status, accomplishments, hobbies, skills, and belongings – exists for the sole purpose of enabling and supporting the network of relationships in your life. Nobody gets to the end of life and wishes they'd spent more time at work. Instead, we treasure the memories surrounding the relationships that enhance our lives and give us purpose and meaning. And if we

> **A blueprint for your important relationships can help ensure that you give them the proper attention they need to bring lifelong fulfillment.**

hustle for money, we invariably do so with the idea that it will put us in a better position to pursue our most desired relationships and the experiences together that we most cherish. Somehow, we all sense that our connections with other people have an enduring quality. They seem to live on beyond this life. Or at least, they take priority over day-to-day matters. Creating a blueprint for your important relationships can help you ensure that you give them the proper attention they need to bring lifelong fulfillment.

CAREER

You probably don't need to be prodded about setting career goals or maximizing your career potential. In fact, there's a better chance you'd need the opposite. The tendency is to emphasize this area at the expense of the others. Creating a blueprint for your career enables you to identify precisely how it can benefit your life – or in some cases derail it. I want my career to add value to my life as a venue for exercising my skills and pursuing my interests. I don't want my career to cause conflict with my family, or to become the all-consuming dictator of my life. My career blueprint helps me to assess these factors regularly, to set goals, and to make adjustments. Again, if the goal is to cultivate a sense of rich that lasts forever, it can't be inextricably linked to a career that only lasts forty years or so. What happens when you retire? Does happiness retire with it? Or do you scramble to cultivate the art of happiness from another source? Career is part of the picture. But it's not the whole thing. In a nutshell,

> **Your career should enable your life's purpose or "calling".**

your career should enable your life's purpose or "calling". If you miss your purpose, you'll never have the joy and fulfillment you were created to enjoy, no matter how much you accomplish in your career.

PHYSICAL

These days, it seems like people are either fitness fanatics or they just try not to think about it. One thing is clear: the economy of food is driving more and more people to consume more calories than they need. Food manufacturers and restaurants not only market aggressively, they offer bigger and bigger portions to stay competitive with the trend toward "value" menus. Meanwhile, technology invents more and more ways for us to stay sedentary no matter how busy life gets. Unless you follow a plan for your physical fitness, most people will gain a few pounds every year. Play that out over a decade or two, and you've not only got a significant weight problem on your hands, you're also prone to the ailments that wait for anyone who slows down too much. The old saying goes that if you've got your health, you've got everything. And if that's the case, fewer and fewer people have as much as they could. I don't want to become a slave to the gym. But I do want to enjoy the full riches of health available to me. And that means crafting a blueprint that will keep me at a level of fitness that feels good and promotes longevity.

SPIRITUAL

Research has long held that people are more fulfilled when their lives include some expression of spirituality. Whether it's a formal religion, or a personal practice with spiritual overtones, like yoga, it is recognized in professional circles as a key to happiness. So the idea of holistic riches must include this category. In fact, some would argue that it's the most important, as it determines how we function in all the other categories. At any rate, there's something to this aspect of life that can't be ignored. Whether you're a religious person or not, you have a spiritual side that requires attention to be at your best. And rather than just feeling whatever spirituality comes naturally, I have an intentional plan – a blueprint – for exploiting all that this dimension of life is meant to be.

Notice that four of the five categories above have almost nothing to do with money. And yet they have everything to do with a sense of being "rich". That means no matter what your financial status, virtually everyone has the ability become "rich" in these areas. When you break life down into these five categories, the conversation about "rich" is quickly separated from the topic of money. And that's an important thing to understand. Being rich isn't entirely a matter of building financial equity. It requires attention to your equity in these other categories. Since there are some things money can't buy, then having all the money in the world can't guarantee you will be "rich".

> **Since there are some things money can't buy, then having all the money in the world can't guarantee you will be "rich".**

For some people, that poses serious problems. Investing money is straightforward. But what do you plunk down if you want to make an investment in one of those other categories?

If there are some things money can't buy, then what *can* you use to buy them?

In the previous chapter, I started wrestling with that issue out loud. As the money fluctuated, I saw firsthand how spending power fluctuates with it. But I was also reminded of just how many things money can't buy in the first place. This journey brought me full-circle to the issue of where life's purchasing power really comes from. Money is one type. But it's only part of the story.

If you think about it, this can really turn your personal economy on its head. First of all, we're saying that money isn't the only asset worth acquiring. Nor is it the only form of currency that can be traded for other assets. In fact, it's just one of three that I know of. The other two are Time and Talent. And they are more powerful and precious than money. Because their potential far surpasses any dollar figure we could assign to them. Money, for the most part, is actually just a reflection of the other two universal resources – time and talent. Now let me explain what I mean by that.

Bill Gates started with a talent; then he invested massive amounts of time in it; and the billions of dollars that followed are nothing but a reflection representing the value of his talent and the value of his time. He's financially super-rich now. But there was a time when all he had was a dream, some talent, and a season of life – time – to pursue his dream. You see, when we tell the story in retrospect, we often focus on how rich they are now. And in the process, we downplay the fact that it was really the talent and the time that led to all the money.

This can be bittersweet news. Bitter news for anyone who's accumulated truckloads of money while going bankrupt in any of the other four categories. And sweet news for anyone who thought they'd never have enough money to be rich. As it turns out, two-thirds of what you need to purchase these kinds of riches were given to you as a birthright. Everybody comes into the world with a measure of talent. And everybody receives an allotment of time in which to use it.

> **All forms of currency in the world fit neatly into three universal categories: Time, Talent, and Treasure.**

If you think about it, all forms of currency in the world fit neatly into those three universal categories: Time, Talent, and Treasure.

When we talk about the idea of holistic riches, we're essentially recognizing that money isn't the only thing that holds value. And here, now, we have a list of all the possible ways to add value in those areas. If the "The Big 5" categories are the engines that produce happiness, then Time, Talent, and Treasure are the gas we put in the tank. Invested wisely, these resources will increase the equity you enjoy in any one of these Big 5 accounts.

That's why happiness is available regardless of a person's financial situation. And it's why being "rich" (i.e. happy and fulfilled, with a life of purpose) is so often not tied to finances. Even if you don't have much treasure, you've got the same amount of time each day as everyone else. And in the right circumstances, you might also have a unique talent that can add to your investment in one of these areas.

And as we're about to see, maximum wealth is not so much about building excess in any one of these areas as it is what you do with it once you have it.

Chapter 9

THE SINKING VALUE OF A DOLLAR

At the end of 2009, the Tongil Market in Pyongyang, North Korea became a ghost town. Normally bustling with activity, the shops fell strangely silent. The retail displays were full of goods to sell. And many of the locals had plenty of cash to spend. However, nobody was buying.

The reason? Cash had lost its value.

In a surprise announcement, the North Korean government had declared a new standard for its currency. The old one was retired immediately. And while citizens could trade their cash for new currency, the exchange rate was one penny on the dollar. In effect, cash was useless.

This was especially bad news for those who had faithfully saved for the future. And there were many who fit that description. Despite hoarding piles of cash at home, many people found themselves unable to put food on the table. And reports of suicides soon followed as hopelessness spread through the marketplace.

> The more cash you have in your bank account, the less value your money brings you in return.

It's easy to understand how a dollar loses value when the currency is retired. But that's not the only way your dollars can shrink. In fact, the more cash you have in your bank account, the less value your money brings you in return. Allow me to explain.

Early in life, you discover that you can trade a coin or a dollar for something you want. It's our first lesson in economics. We might not understand the details – like why a nickel is so much bigger than a dime, but only half as valuable. But we make the connection that somehow, these little denominations of money hold the key to satisfying some basic needs and wants.

From there, it's off to the races. If money is the key to all those other things, then our assignment is pretty simple: Get money.

Even the most remedial thinkers in our culture seem to grasp this concept. But ironically, everybody – from the simplest to the smartest – seems to lose that original connection that money is only as good as what you trade it for. We trade it for meals. We trade it for houses and cars. And in the process, we manage to acquire all the things we need to maintain a certain quality of life.

But what happens when your wealth exceeds what is needed for those basic things? Do you trade the excess for an additional meal? You've only got one stomach. Do you trade it for another house and another car? You can only sleep in one place or drive one car at a time. Sure you can

> **Money is only as good as what you trade it for.**

get a nicer version of everything. You can even get two or three houses with multiple cars for each.

But here's the problem. The richer you get, the less value those things really give you back in return. And this principle is not only true for your monetary treasure, but it's also true for the other two forms of "riches" you possess: time and talent.

To demonstrate this principle further, imagine three of the thickest, juiciest steaks in the world are served up in front of you right now. These are the really big ones like you'd expect from the finest steak houses. All three are identical. And all three are the tastiest cuisine available anywhere. As you sink your teeth into the first one, the value it brings is high. Not only is it satisfying your basic need for sustenance, but it's also pleasing your palate at the same time.

As you bite into the second one, the experience is somehow a little different. The pleasure is still high. But your hunger is no longer in the ravenous category. It's not that the steak is any less able to satisfy, it's just that the need for satisfaction has already been met by the first one. So the second one, by default, is unable to deliver at quite the same level of the first. It's not that it wasn't as good. They were identical. The value is different because your need was different. Having had your need for sustenance met already, the second steak represented a luxury – an indulgence above and beyond your most basic needs.

Now start into the third steak and the value it brings is even lower. At this point, your stomach is starting to bulge. Instead of enjoying the experience, you now must "work" to down the serving. As you chew each bite, your jaw muscles might begin to ache. The texture seems different, and the meat no longer melts in your mouth. With each swallow, you begin to feel your gag reflex kicking in. Again, this steak is identical to the other two, but because your situation is now different – your primary needs are already met – the value you receive from it has been greatly reduced. In fact, it has the potential to make you throw up the whole meal!

That's the way it is with anything of value. The more abundant it becomes, the less value it represents to the possessor.

That first $30,000 car is worth every penny you pay for it. It gives you the ability to travel anywhere you need to go, the convenience of going whenever you want, and it gives you better access to the job that provides money for the car and all the other expenses you encounter. In fact, you might even say that car has even more value to you than the $30,000 you shelled out for it. That helps explain why it feels so good to drive it home for the first time.

But put an additional $30,000 into your vehicle budget – either for a second car, or a more luxurious one – and you'll get a lot less back from each dollar. You might not mind too much. But the economic reality holds true. Twice the money won't give you twice the ability to travel, nor will it give you twice the convenience. Sure, it gives you

THE SINKING VALUE OF A DOLLAR

some value. But you'd have to admit it's nowhere near as high as the value of going from no car to having a car.

The same is true for houses. The greatest value lies in the prospect of getting a roof over your head. But once you've accomplished that mission, the rest are conveniences and cosmetics. And as nice as those things are, they still can't rival the value of having the more basic need for shelter met.

So here's the dilemma with great wealth. As you move up Maslow's Hierarchy from the basic necessities like survival needs and creature comforts up toward wants and luxuries, the actual value to you personally goes down. Give $1,000 to a homeless man and the value is enormous. But give $1,000 to Bill Gates and the additional value to him personally is almost nothing. He already has the things $1,000 will buy. And it's not enough of an increase to move the meter much in his life. It might even represent a bit of a nuisance, necessitating an unplanned trip to the bank to make a deposit.

I call this principle the Law of Diminishing Value of Wealth. And this helps to explain why money falls short in the end. It's not that it holds no value. But the role money plays in a person's life shifts at a certain point. Once you meet your own basic necessities, the value of money is greatest elsewhere. While it still holds the same

> **Once you meet your own basic necessities, the value of money is greatest elsewhere.**

value out in the world, it diminishes tremendously the minute you lay your hands on it. I'm not sure if there's a formula for it, but your second million is worth a fraction of your first, and your third is a fraction of your second, and so on.

Maybe you've felt that gut-wrenching emptiness I'm talking about.

When you got your first job, you probably used to dream of making "real money" some day. Think back for a moment. I'm not saying you weren't also glad to have a job. But did you ever used to fantasize about making the big bucks? Most people can remember a dream number they longed to hit one day. Maybe it was hitting six figures. Or perhaps it was even higher. No doubt it was a number that would have comfortably eclipsed all your monthly needs and wants.

Now here's a telltale question. Do you still have those same kinds of thoughts today? The numbers might be different. But when was the last time you thought of a number that's higher than your current earnings? In the last year? The last month? This week?

> **The role money plays in your life actually shifts. If your use of money doesn't shift with it, the value you get in return feels emptier and emptier.**

Here's my point. For most people, that's a perennial reality. No matter how high we climb on the financial ladder, there's always another rung. And it's not just coming from our honorable ambition to be as productive and accomplished as we can be in life. To some degree, there's an element of dissatisfaction with our current station. We're actually unhappy. We've had dozens of raises over the years – perhaps doubled our salary several times over – and yet we can still lament that it's not enough. If only we had a little bit more.

That's the Law of Diminishing Value of Wealth at work. The role money plays in your life actually shifts. And if your use of money doesn't shift along with it, then the value you get back in return feels emptier and emptier.

But it doesn't have to be this way.

If the value of money can change depending on who's holding it or how much you already have, then money isn't really our ultimate currency. I believe it's only our currency while we're working to meet our basic needs. But once those are addressed, the real basis of value in life shifts to another treasure, and then another, and so on. As it turns out, the gold standard only applies when it comes to obtaining food, shelter, transportation, and the like.

> **If the value of money can change depending on who's holding it or how much you already have, then money isn't really our ultimate currency.**

If you think about it, our idea of currency is relative. In fact, there are three different stages of "rich" that a person can experience in life. And in order to minimize the diminishing value of your various riches, there are specific ways you should allocate your riches depending on the stage you're in. The value of clean water is viewed different in a third-world country than it is in a superpower. Similarly, the value of the things you possess – time, talent, and treasure – changes as your situation in life changes.

For simplicity, let me suggest three basic ways, or stages, people allocate their resources.

The first stage is Sustenance. When you don't know where your next meal is coming from, the basic need for money for survival is everything. The value of those first dollars is set by what it must buy: food, shelter, and clothing. The question of sustenance – or basic provisions – must be answered by everyone.

As you move up the scale beyond abject poverty, though, your focus begins to shift to factors that impact quality-of-life. "Dollar impact" gives way to the impact of things like additional choices, enriching relationships, and experiences that expand your horizons. That's the second stage – Luxuries.

Move up further, and an interesting thing happens. Rather than simply slide the scale to bigger ticket versions of everything – a bigger car, house etc. – the next source of value comes from the promise of autonomy. Autonomy – the freedom to come and go as you please – is a core pursuit of the human soul. It is the opposite of slavery. Just as the stomach aches for food, the soul aches for freedom. And the ultimate promise of money is that it can actually deliver this dream. That's the third stage – freedom.

Many people get stuck in stage two when their desire for freedom takes a back seat to the pursuit of more and more luxuries. Basic laziness can also prevent a person from progressing to the next level. When either of these issues prevails, our pursuit of freedom suffers neglect.

Think back to your first job again for a moment. In the early days, your money automatically went toward sustenance. Similarly, your first few financial growth spurts went toward choices and luxuries. But the shift to autonomy is not as natural for most. It requires that you decide how much luxury you really need before you'd rather have financial independence instead. The commercials will try to convince you there's always one more thing to acquire first. But if you follow their suggestions to the point of denying yourself some financial freedom, those luxuries will bring less and less satisfaction.

Therefore, this succession of stages is not as intuitive as one might think. In particular, countless achievers fail to make the all-important shift from the second stage, luxuries, to the third, financial freedom. Rather than allocating their resources to purchase their own autonomy, they simply buy more and more expensive versions of the things they already possess. In the process, they expend great effort and deplete vast resources but don't find themselves significantly happier. And when they're not, they wonder why.

As you move through these stages, it's as if the very basis of currency changes along the way. The Currency of Sustenance refers to the stage in which dollars have their maximum value as a means to acquire the basic things we need to survive. The second stage sees a shift toward the Currency of Luxuries; the term "discretionary" is sometimes used to describe this stage in which a dollar is most valuable as a device for attaining an improved quality-of-life. In the third stage, the basis of currency shifts toward Freedom, referring to the stage in which a dollar is most rewarding when it provides an income and delivers personal autonomy. In this case, dollars are leveraged for their unique ability to produce more dollars through investments, thereby offering a self-perpetuating flow of cash that funds levels one and two continuously.

I should point out that stages two and three are often perceived to be interchangeable, depending on what the individual values most. For example, some people would rather forgo all forms of luxury in order to achieve financial independence, free from the necessity of working for pay. This would be the person who lives the most meager of lifestyles, yet has a nest egg earning enough interest to pay the bills. Arguably, though, even this person has spent something toward quality-of-life, as there is no tangible way to distinguish the bare minimum from slight improvements to that minimum. In other words, what one man claims is basic provision; another might consider to be a luxury. As such, virtually everyone observes these three stages in the same order.

My point in laying out these three different ways a dollar can have value is to convince you that there's more to money than money. In the same way, there's more to rich than rich. Money is just the veneer – the visible representative of all the things that hold tangible value. And those things vary from situation to situation. To a homeless beggar, "rich" means never having to worry about the next meal. To the middle class, "rich" means never having to work again. And that's just the beginning of the list of definitions that exist for "rich".

Now think back to the Big 5 categories we referred to as "holistic riches". As you notice, the more money you amass, the smaller the role it plays in creating an experience that qualifies as "rich", and the more crucial it becomes to establish balance between the categories. That's because, as we just said, there's more to money than money.

What's really important is the way money enhances the holistic picture of life.

Now, having said all that, there's a fourth stage beyond those three. And it doesn't always come in order. But it impacts the way a dollar has value in another way altogether. For many, it represents the highest value a dollar can bring to the bearer. In fact, it's so important to our discussion of cultivating the experience of being "rich", it deserves its own chapter.

> There's a fourth stage beyond those three. For many, it represents the highest value a dollar can bring to the bearer.

Chapter 10

THE TRANSCENDENT VALUE OF A DOLLAR

I should point out that while the three "stages" we described previously often come in order, the fourth one doesn't really fit in a single place on that timeline. It can be experienced at any point, regardless of your circumstances. So while I refer to it as the fourth stage – and it clearly represents yet another basis of currency – it actually has the potential to encompass all three of the others.

I call this fourth dimension Transcendence, or the Currency of Transcendence. In this stage, a dollar has maximum value to a person when it is applied toward transcendent things – initiatives, accomplishments, or causes that bring significance to the person's life, such as creating a legacy or contributing to the common good of the world. This category includes basically anything that expresses your purpose in life or that lives beyond you.

> **A dollar has maximum value to a person when it is applied toward transcendent things**

Regardless of your financial stage in life, you can experience a perspective which holds that your dollars will never give you more in return than when they're spent toward some purpose that gives a greater sense of meaning to your life. It's probably true that most people reach this point after meeting their own basic needs first, and perhaps after indulging in a few luxuries too, but it's not always the case. Someone with strong humanitarian values will likely forgo his own luxuries and move immediately to applying his time, talent, and monetary resources toward the pursuit of transcendent things. For that matter, there are examples of people who spend themselves in the name of transcendence even at the expense of their basic needs. Think of Mahatma Gandhi staging a "sit-in", for example.

Let's go back to the example of the three steaks for a moment. What if, instead of trying to force down that third beautiful steak yourself, you had shared it with someone else? It could be someone you love. Or it could be someone in need of sustenance. Either way, it represents an investment in something transcendent – something that has meaning beyond yourself. In essence, you trade your own physical experience for the opportunity to create an experience for someone else. And in the case of the third steak, it's a definite improvement as you trade the negative physical experience of being over-stuffed for the positive experience it brings to someone else.

This is the principle I was missing when I declared my own "retirement" at age 30. As I churned through my daily routine of visiting the gym and sitting by the pool, the futility of it all was asphyxiating. Despite having my dream marriage, dream car, and dream situation, I wasn't receiving a value in life that was worthy of the kind of money I was dealing with. No matter how much "richer" I got, the perceived value of those dollars kept sinking lower and lower. It was miserable.

> No matter how much "richer" I got, the perceived value of those dollars kept sinking lower and lower. It was miserable.

On paper, I had already moved through the first three stages. I had basic provisions for sustenance, I had discretionary options and luxuries, and I had the autonomy of financial freedom. But I wasn't really using what I possessed – time, talent, or treasure – toward this fourth category. Instead, I just kept adding to the pile and wondering why it seemed so meaningless. And the more I added, each dollar – or hour of free time – meant less and less, because of the Law of Diminishing Value of Wealth.

We've all heard that money doesn't guarantee happiness. I was already familiar with the phrase. But nobody had ever explained why. Eventually I realized that having money wasn't being rich. And just buying things wasn't being rich. And being free to come and go as I pleased wasn't rich either.

The full experience of being rich must also include this fourth stage. A person is not fully rich until he enjoys the rich experience of making a difference beyond himself – either by providing for the

> **A person is not fully rich until he enjoys the rich experience of making a difference beyond himself.**

needs of someone else, or contributing to an effort that benefits the common good. There's something about knowing that you've left the world a better place that holds intrinsic value. And the basic equation behind that feeling is to spend yourself in some way on the world at large.

Moreover, it seems to be a dynamic that it must cost you personally if it is to bring satisfaction. To some degree, the more it costs, the more satisfaction it brings – assuming it is given freely and without compulsion, not out of guilt or obligation.

If we observe these four stages that impact our time, talent, and treasure, it's possible to get a lot more value in return whenever we spend them. "Rich" is a fragile state that comes and goes depending on whether we observe the Law of Diminishing Value of Wealth. A minimum wage worker can experience "rich" by putting food on the table consistently. He feels even richer when he acquires the ability to eat out at a nice restaurant. Another level of rich may come when he can buy a house, provide for his family, and save for retirement.

But here's where "rich" becomes elusive for most people. Despite his rising income, there's only so many luxurious upgrades that can truly satisfy. Eventually, he can't experience happiness unless he applies those resources toward some degree of autonomy. If he buys himself some freedom, the sensation of "rich" continues. If he simply adds more luxuries, he can actually feel enslaved by them. And ultimately, yet another level of wealth won't feel richer unless it is leveraged toward this fourth category of value – transcendence.

This explains why happiness often seems unrelated to wealth, and why people say things like, "Rich is a state of mind." And it's why we conclude that the whole subject is relative. You don't have to be financially wealthy to start building value in this category.

In my case, the additional money I made – beyond the wealth that provided my autonomy – felt useless until I started to leverage it as a tool for experiencing meaning and purpose in life.

I see a lot of wealthy people stumbling across this principle eventually. Sooner or later, an accountant or a bookkeeper mentions the value of setting up a foundation or using charitable giving to offset a tax liability. But even though the benefactor probably gets a warm, fuzzy feeling inside, it's not always the same as feeling rich. You can always tell when a wealthy person is just dabbling with warm fuzzies and when he falls in love with this unexpected source of joy. It feels like hitting the jackpot of finding meaning and purpose for their wealth.

Let's look at the former case. When a person's experience with this level of value is random, they tend to alternate between charitable interests and their own interests. From time to time, the extra wealth they acquire results in some additional attention to a humanitarian cause or their favorite foundation. They don't go overboard, though. They balance their outside contributions with a few indulgences of their own. They purchase occasional luxuries and take various trips as if to maintain a steady supply of satisfaction from life. Their investments in "meaning" are just one more activity in the smorgasbord of functions designed to create a rich life experience. But they're not the centerpiece. They represent just a fraction of how these incremental dollars are allocated. In the end, most of it goes into either stage-two purchases – additional luxuries – or stage three – additional net worth to pad their financial freedom. As a result, the rich experience of transcendence is not completely missed, but it's certainly not leveraged for its maximum potential. If only this person understood that untold fulfillment is available by carefully allocating wealth in observance of these four stages.

In contrast, now consider the latter case – the person who discovers something that brings maximum potential value from this incremental wealth. To this person, the additional value of finding and expressing life's purpose and meaning is undeniable. They come away from the experience having never encountered anything like making an impact in the world. Everything else that money can buy pales in comparison. No purchase they've ever made has come close to delivering the feeling of satisfaction that comes from discovering their place in the universe as a person who meets the needs of other people. From that point forward, there is a new standard for fulfillment. Dollars spent on anything less than this value are wasted. You can see them throwing themselves into this area of interest more and more. Oftentimes, the media looks on with curiosity as these people seem to withdraw from high society in order to become devoted to what appears to be selfless abandonment. But it's really the ultimate thrill for the benefactor.

For example, consider the founder of one of the most successful carpet companies in the world. Beginning from scratch, with just a few inventions, he knew what it meant to provide for his basic needs.

As the company took off, he began to afford some long-awaited luxuries. Eventually, he had more money than he could spend in a lifetime. At that point, he could afford to do whatever he desired with his days. About that time, he discovered the experience of transcendence. As the general awareness of ecological issues rose everywhere, he began to see that his own company and industry were contributing to the pollution of the planet. From then on he has spent tremendous amounts of his time and money not only to reverse his own legacy, but with the goal of leaving the world even cleaner than he found it. In short, the fulfillment he gets from allocating his resources toward this transcendent goal is far more satisfying than any new yacht, vacation home, or private jet he could purchase. Likewise, he wouldn't find more joy from personal conquests like climbing the world's tallest peaks, winning an Olympic medal, or being the first to row around the world in a canoe.

Here's my conclusion. In the pursuit of becoming "rich" most of us get caught up in these first three stages; all the while, one of the most rewarding dimensions of rich is waiting to be experienced by everyone – regardless of your level of provision, the luxuries you've acquired, or the freedom you've attained. Think of people like Mother Theresa, who skipped right past the first three stages of wealth and essentially existed in the fourth alone. To her, there was no greater value than transcendent achievements like giving of herself to others. She didn't wait until "retirement" when she could afford to work as a volunteer. She went right for it.

Similarly, there are many "millionaires" who fit the same description. Industrialist Milton Scott lived to be more than 100 years old in the same un-air-conditioned house he built for his wife in sweltering

Atlanta, GA. He kept four suits and worked well into his nineties. While he spent almost nothing on himself – even his retirement savings were meager – year after year throughout his life, he gave millions to needy orphans and other humanitarian causes around the world. Like Mother Theresa and many others, Scott preferred the pleasure of accomplishing transcendent things more than a table full of steaks.

> **The ultimate thrill awaits if we can just make the transition to this fourth category of dollar-value.**

Sooner or later, we get our fill of new things, new places, and new thrills. Granted, that process can be a lot of fun while it lasts. But those thrills can actually run out even if the money doesn't. And unless we understand these stages of allocation, we can end up in the peculiar category of people who have everything they want except the happiness they so desperately need. Meanwhile, the ultimate thrill awaits if we can just make the transition to this fourth category of dollar-value.

Rather than waiting to experience this randomly, I've taken some cues from several of these examples I've mentioned and adopted a financial model that guarantees the maximum value in return for every dollar. I've drawn a line – for me – for each of these four levels of currency, or dollar-value. I've pre-decided how much I can spend on luxuries and still get back the greatest value in return. I've pre-decided how much I need in order to ensure autonomy. And the rest, I've pre-decided to allocate toward things that express my purpose in life. That not only gives me a sense of meaning, it also guarantees that I'm getting the most out of every dollar I touch.

As I mentioned, the first three stages of dollar-value are usually observed in order. But this fourth category doesn't always come fourth. It can be third, second, or even first. When people sacrifice personal freedom, personal comforts, or basic needs for the sake of a significant cause, in effect they put this category ahead of others. It might be a wealthy philanthropist with a modest lifestyle, or a struggling mother who uses her last dollar to feed her child instead of herself, essentially skipping right past the other three categories to get to the transcendent goal of feeding her child. In either case, their dollars realized their maximum value when they were used, not for the possessor's own luxury, but for the benefit of others. In return, they fulfilled a sense of duty to the larger world around them, even though it came at the expense of their own luxury.

> **Sometimes giving something away brings more value to us than keeping it.**

The question for all of us is whether something truly holds value if it isn't held by us personally. Sometimes giving something away brings more value to us than keeping it. That's the difference between personal value and common value. When we give generously, we share in the common value of something even if we aren't the direct beneficiary of the primary value.

These four stages or categories challenge us to move beyond a mindset of ownership and into a mindset of stewardship. Ownership entices us to hoard up things for ourselves. Stewardship gives us the satisfaction of sharing things with others; and when we do, we create and sustain maximum value in the things we give away. When you step back and objectify the value of something – looking at it in terms of the value it carries regardless of who owns it – it suggests different things about how it should be used.

When it comes to cultivating a sense of peace and fulfillment in life, I've found that this distinction between ownership and stewardship plays an important role. The mindset of ownership tends to generate stress and despair as we struggle in vain to keep the world around us from losing value. The mindset of stewardship, on the other hand, promotes a sense of satisfaction that comes from knowing we fulfilled the inner longing we all share to create value and sustain value in the things we touch. It leaves us feeling a general sense of hope in the world around us. That positive report on our extended surroundings does more for our well-being than the most extravagant luxuries purchased for the smaller arena of self.

I'll come back to this subject in the following pages. But first I want to retrace the steps we've taken so far. Where have we been? And where does all this leave us?

Originally, I set out to identify and describe some key principles for this idea of being rich forever. That sounds simple enough. However, we soon discovered that "rich" is a wildly dynamic concept. As we saw, it means different things to different people. In addition, it means different things depending on your circumstances. As a result, we've ended up describing "rich" like some sort of elusive paradox of illusions. It sounds like one of those lofty parables – like letting go of something you love in order to obtain it.

But as theoretical as all this sounds, I'm more interested in the very practical implications it holds for us. What does it look like to allocate one's riches – time, talent, and treasure – according to these four categories? And what does it look like when we stray from that plan?

Does it really matter if I don't observe these stages deliberately? Can it really keep me from feeling rich?

Or, perhaps more importantly, is there really a connection between "rich" and "happy" anyway? After all, happiness is ultimately what we hope to gain from wealth.

To explore these questions further, I'd like to introduce you to the richest man in history.

What if that connection can't be trusted after all?

To explore these questions further, I'd like to introduce you to the richest man in history.

Chapter 11

SOLOMON'S SECRET

Ponder this question for a moment: If you could be rich in all the ways we've described so far, would you be happy?

That sounds simple enough, doesn't it? It's such an obvious question, you're probably ready with an answer before you even finish reading it. After all, isn't that the point of this whole discussion? Isn't this entire book based on the assumption that everyone wants to be rich… so they can be happy?

But I want to reexamine this basic premise.

What if being rich, the way we've described it, isn't all it's cracked up to be? I know, I know… you don't care if it doesn't solve *all* your problems. You'd be just fine with that little disappointment. At least it would solve *most* of them, right?

But I want to challenge your assumptions here. What if the "rich" scenario you're picturing for yourself has a huge hole in it? What if, in your pursuit of being rich, you're overlooking a key aspect of happiness? And what if by focusing on your newly refined definition of rich, you somehow neglect to give proper attention to something else – something that was essential to the pursuit of happiness?

As we've seen, unless you understand the four stages of money and the different ways to allocate your resources for each, you might become wealthy beyond your dreams and yet never be quite satisfied. What if, as that suggests, "rich" is not synonymous with "happy" at all?

I want to go out on a limb here and suggest that it's actually not. I'll admit that being rich can almost always bring some form of pleasure, the same way a sugar cube tastes sweet melting on your tongue, or a cool breeze brings relief on a hot day. But what if there's more to good nutrition than a cube of sugar? What if pursuing the pleasures of being rich in all the ways we've described still leaves you deprived of some essential ingredients to experiencing a life that fills you with happiness?

I think of the lab rats who consistently choose a diet of flavored water over nutrient-rich pellets, despite their slow death by malnutrition. Or the meth addict who, having experienced the intense high of this drug of choice, will allow the destruction of everything he holds dear in order to reach that state again and again. Is it possible for us to be so enraptured by pleasurable experiences we call "rich" that we could end up devoid of the essential ingredients for happiness? I'll be honest. Money enables some intense highs. Making a million dollars on a phone call on the deck of a yacht feels incredible. And having experienced such things, I could see spending the rest of my life in a cycle of earn-spend-enjoy that simply escalates over time. But what if all along true happiness were the product of a different pursuit altogether? One that was within our grasp almost from the start? One that can be grasped by everyone, not just those with large bank accounts.

> **What if "rich" is not synonymous with "happy" at all? What if all along true happiness were the product of a different pursuit altogether?**

Consider these names: Bernie Madoff. Tiger Woods. Michael Vick. Lindsey Lohan. Howard Hughes. Michael Jackson. Anna Nicole Smith. Mike Tyson. You get the idea; go ahead and add your own list of names to this one. I'm not saying these people weren't happy. But being rich, by itself, has been a pretty poor guarantor of happiness for those people. And it hasn't prevented train wrecks for any of them. In some cases, there's even an inverse relationship between their wealth and their happiness. The richer they are, the harder they fall.

Now maybe you've heard this age-old argument all your life. And it's no secret that money can't buy happiness. But the reason I mention it here is that I take a slightly different view from the conventional theory about money and happiness. I believe money plays a huge role in the happiness equation. And I think most of the go-to "moral" arguments on the subject have glossed over this important truth in the past. In our haste to acknowledge that rich people are often unhappy, we've carelessly dismissed the role that money does

> **The secret lies more in *what you do with money* than in *how much you possess*.**

play in bringing happiness. We've thrown the baby out with the bathwater. So don't throw away your money just yet. Possessing great riches may not be the lone key to happiness. But it's definitely useful. And as I hope to convince you, the secret lies more in *what you do with money* than in *how much you possess.*

Rich people aren't rich because they *have* things like treasure, time, and talent. They're rich – i.e. happy – because of how they *allocate* those things.

To explore my theory, I want to introduce you to the wealthiest man who ever lived. Forget Bill Gates or Warren Buffet. Let's go all the way to the top of the list. There, according to many respected authorities, we find the man who's held the number one spot for more than three thousand years. No one has surpassed him yet. Nor do we know of anyone in recorded history before him whose wealth was greater. He was King Solomon of Israel.

Not only is Solomon believed to have had more wealth than all the other examples we could choose, he also wrote extensively about his experiences with it. So we're left with an excellent case study of the relationship between *rich* and *happy.*

One of the most valuable aspects of Solomon's example is the insight we get into the mind of the mega-rich. Few people have been so candid on such a public level. Many have shared the glitzy side of wealth. But Solomon offers his most basic emotions, unedited, for the world to see. Unabashedly, he recounts the extreme pleasure of fulfilling his wildest dreams. And he mourns out loud the realization that some of his most basic needs can't be resolved with any amount of money.

You see, the minute we learn that somebody's rich, we instantly think of them differently. We think they're nothing like us. *They're rich*, we think. So therefore, their entire world is completely different from ours. Right? And in the process of making such assumptions, we miss some of the real lessons we could learn from their lives.

Instead of seeing yourself as different from the mega-wealthy, you should think of yourself as just one or two lottery tickets shy of Bill Gates. A few billion dollars ago, Bill Gates was just a guy just like you, wrestling with whether he can really afford a new couch or if he should stick with the old one a while longer. Likewise, a few billion dollars from now, you'd be wrestling with what to do with all your resources now that you've acquired them. And in reality, that's the thing you should be wrestling with already – whether we're talking about $100 dollars or $100 billion dollars. If you got a chance to chat with Bill Gates or Warren Buffet, they might tell you the same thing themselves. Life's not really that different just because you have money. In the meantime, we can find these insights between the lines of Solomon's life.

According to some of our best historical documents, Israel's King Solomon had more going on in our first three stages of "rich" than anyone before or since. His basic needs were virtually guaranteed for life. He enjoyed every form of luxury imaginable. And his days were his to spend as he wished. Yet somehow, unthinkably, the secret to happiness eluded him. Here was a man who had wealth, health, family, and religion. But when you read his own accounts, it's obvious that this richest man in the world was also one of the poorest in terms of happiness. Was this the earliest recorded case of clinical depression? No doubt we'd try him on anti-depressants today. But most likely, he was simply facing the same realities that await all of us as we learn the ins and outs of handling time, talent, and treasure.

Just to put this in perspective, let me compare his lifestyle and net worth in today's terms.

In the matter of sustenance, or the first stage of wealth, Solomon was as assured of the basic essentials as anyone could be in this life. As the king over the preeminent superpower of the time, he enjoyed unmatched job security – a lifelong contract with an enormous salary. He had stores of gold and silver saved up for those rainy days too. In addition, he never felt threatened by changing tax laws or millage rate hikes. He was the final voice on such matters and could decree anything he wished. To say the least, food, shelter, and clothing were Solomon's with endless redundancies. And in the unlikely event that his own provisions somehow failed him, the favor of all his subjects would have come to his support.

As for luxuries, or our second stage of wealth, Solomon left us detailed records of his indulgences. For starters, we know something about the size of his estate. Although it's hard to translate the value of gold into modern US currency with exact precision, most scholars estimate his base annual salary at more than half a billion dollars. Per year, that is. In addition, ancient records indicate gifts of gold from neighboring countries totaling nearly 100,000 pounds. At today's prices, let's just say that much treasure would be somewhere in the billions.

But gold was just the beginning. Solomon also owned 12,000 horses, 1,400 chariots, and vast stores of ivory, spices, and precious stones. He controlled palaces, cities, and collected a portion of all trade between countries to the north and south. Suffice it to say he was loaded.

And he took full advantage of it too. Unlike Scrooge, who hoarded everything, Solomon lavished every conceivable perk on himself. He put it rather bluntly: "All that my eyes desired I did not refuse them. I did not withhold my heart from any pleasure."

> "All that my eyes desired I did not refuse them. I did not withhold my heart from any pleasure."

One can only imagine what Solomon really meant by a statement like that. That is, until you read his line-by-line account of the ways he indulged himself: "I built houses for myself, I planted vineyards for myself; I made gardens and parks for myself and I planted in them all kinds of fruit trees; I made ponds of water for myself from which to irrigate a forest of growing trees. I bought male and female slaves and I had homeborn slaves. Also I possessed flocks and herds larger than all who preceded me in Jerusalem. Also, I collected for myself silver and gold and the treasure of kings and provinces. I provided for myself male and female singers and the pleasures of men--many concubines." For the record, the official number of Solomon's concubines was 300. And lest we misinterpret that little indicator of his appetite for gratification, it is also reported that he had seven hundred wives as well. Needless to say, the guy knew how to indulge himself.

As a man of means, Solomon had no trouble accomplishing our

third stage of wealth as well – the total freedom to come and go as he pleased. As we just saw in his own words, he was a full-time pleasure-seeker. It's not like he had to work until closing time before he could play. Unlike most people, Solomon was not working for the weekend. Every day was his to design as he pleased. In fact, when you combine his wealth with his political power, he was arguably as free to do whatever he wanted as any man who's ever walked the earth.

Finally, to round things out, he had genius. His wisdom is legendary. On numerous occasions his ideas astounded his countrymen. The Queen of Sheba is said to have bestowed enormous gifts of gold on Solomon, all because she was so impressed with the way he responded when she barraged him with deep riddles and trick questions. To say the least, Solomon had a mind that enabled him to succeed in any number of ventures that we might include in our broadest definition of "rich". He was even an accomplished poet and song-writer.

In our culture today, it's hard to picture what it was really like to be Solomon. I guess if you combined the lifestyle of Hugh Heffner, the budget of Bill Gates, the genius of Albert Einstein, the creativity of the Beatles, and the power of the U.S. President, you'd be getting close.

However, in all of the documentation of Solomon's exploits, there is one glaring omission: transcendence. While he writes in great detail of his investments in self-pleasure, we find virtually nothing about his passion to pour into the lives of others. Anecdotally, he had the token accomplishments you'd expect from such a prominent figurehead. He built a temple for the people. He provided the context for a civilization in which everyone lived. And his social machinery included welfare for the needy. For the record, we can say he did quite a bit to leave the world a better place.

But that's where this idea of transcendence is different from token giving. True transcendence involves surrendering a significant portion of your own worldly comfort and pleasure in direct exchange for a greater good. In our best examples of transcendence, we see a disproportionate relationship between taking and giving. It's not a matter of giving ten percent consistently no matter how much you make. Transcendence is what happens when the person realizes that the greatest value is experienced only if those resources are surrendered for the benefit of others. There's a clear cost to the giver. And there's a corresponding joy felt in return.

> **True transcendence involves surrendering a significant portion of your own worldly comfort and pleasure in direct exchange for a greater good.**

If Solomon gave, it doesn't appear that it slowed down his lifestyle much. If giving was his preeminent passion, he sure kept private about it. When it came to the writings in which he poured out his personal emotions, he had plenty to say about his own pleasure. But if he felt strongly about the unending joy of giving to others, it sure got left out of his memoirs. Instead, he seems trapped in a paradigm that knows nothing about the thrill of transcending your own existence through the act of spending yourself – at an actual expense to you personally – for the benefit of something other than you. Compare that to his father's writings in the Psalms, which give us a clear picture of David's personal passion for God and his ways. If transcendence were a passion of Solomon's, you'd expect to find evidence of it somewhere. But his volumes seem fixated only on the theme of personal pleasure.

Ironically, Solomon's runaway desire for pleasure may have kept him from truly enjoying the things he had. Sure enough, he leaves us evidence of the anguish he felt when he concludes, "Vanity, vanity, all is vanity."

I find it interesting that scholars translate "vanity" as "meaningless." As we noted earlier, the quest for meaning is a crucial component of our recipe for the "rich" experience we've so carefully defined. And here, in Solomon's own words, he identifies the one thing that all his full-time pleasure-seeking has failed to produce: meaning.

Now, take yourself back to Solomon's younger days for a moment. Like most of us, he probably had it in the back of his mind that he wanted to be happy someday. And as all people inevitably assume, Solomon envisioned a happiness that included a measure of wealth, a full complement of satisfying relationships, and enough freedom to do the things he wanted to do. In short, Solomon hoped to be "rich". But while most of us hope for it or wish for it, it seems likely that Solomon would have held it as an absolute expectation. After all, he was born into a place of power as a prince. Wealth for him was a certainty, not a distant goal. And with his wisdom and brilliance, he seemed born with an ability to navigate any relationship that was important to him. If anyone held the dream of happiness in the palm of his hand, it was Solomon. He had more treasure, more time, and more talent at his disposal than anyone before or after.

So imagine the sheer angst he must have felt upon finally realizing that it wasn't enough. Despite his unprecedented potential, and his textbook employment of the resources at his disposal, we find him at the end of his life's journey devoid of anything that resembles happy feelings about it. Instead, we find him in agony, expressing hopelessness and despair:

"So I hated life, because the work that is done under the sun was grievous to me. All of it is meaningless, a chasing after the wind. I hated all the things I had toiled for under the sun, because I must leave them to the one who comes after me."

Ecclesiastes 2:17-18

It's as if Solomon's whole life is left as an object lesson for us to observe. He is a living word picture from the past, perfectly crafted to illustrate the message that "rich" does not equal "happy".

So what's the answer, then? If those things fall short, is it really possible that transcendence – our fourth stage – is the key to fulfillment so often overlooked in our quest to be rich and, therefore, happy?

> **Solomon is a living word picture from the past, perfectly crafted to illustrate the message that "rich" does not equal "happy".**

I chose to explore Solomon's life here for the two reasons mentioned. First, he is acknowledged by many to be the richest man who ever lived. Second, he comes with a lengthy diary of personal reflections about the experience of being rich. And now to find the answer to what was a secret for Solomon, I would point to the words of the one person whose wisdom Solomon would have regarded as surpassing even his own. Although Jesus of Nazareth came along hundreds of years after Solomon, he would have been regarded as Solomon's superior in terms of wisdom and understanding. Because of Jesus' spiritual rank, even Solomon would have deferred to his words on the subjects of wealth and happiness. And in fact, Jesus spoke directly about living a rich, purposeful life when he uttered these simple words: "It is more blessed to give than to receive".

> **Jesus spoke directly about living a rich, purposeful life when he uttered these simple words: "It is more blessed to give than to receive".**

In other words, a person who pursues transcendence will be better off than a person who only focuses on getting things for himself.

Sound familiar? In a word: transcendence.

It would be no struggle to pull together a number of similar statements from Jesus that echo this basic idea. In fact, the basic theme of Jesus' life was one of denying self for the benefit of others. Perhaps no quote summarizes this more aptly than when he said, "Give and it will be given unto you, pressed down, shaken together and running over, will men pour into your laps. For with the measure you use, it will be measured back to you".

According to this advice, as well as many other teachings attributed to Jesus, the key to happiness lies not so much in acquiring as it does in what we do with what we've acquired. There's nothing wrong with getting rich. But if you're looking for happiness, just be aware that it's not likely to last unless you also have the right understanding of what to do with riches – big or small – once you obtain them. And paradoxically, the ultimate happiness can only be purchased if we're willing to surrender those sources of happiness that are inferior – personal luxuries, pleasures, and the like – in exchange for the one that comes when we achieve transcendence.

> **But if you're looking for happiness, just be aware that it's not likely to last unless you also have the right understanding of what to do with riches – big or small.**

To make this practical, I've started looking for ways to be a generous person everywhere I go. Not just with money. But a personal "ethos" of generosity. It's letting the other motorist go first, or holding the elevator door even when it's acceptable to act like you didn't know someone else is coming. Sometimes I clear two tables instead of just mine at a fast-food restaurant. And when I find myself in one of those disgusting public restroom, the kind that make you want to avoid touching anything, I had the idea to give it a quick clean-up. Those humbling gestures help train me to the idea of giving to others in varieties of ways. And in the process, I experience more fulfillment than ever.

Perhaps I owe you an explanation for ending up on this subject.

This is a book about being rich forever. So of all things, the last thing you'd expect is a dissertation about giving things away. I chose to write about being rich because I believe that's what most of us know to call it. We say we want to be "rich" because it's generally accepted that having the right things – money, relationships, and freedom – is the key to a happy experience for everyone who has them.

Everyone except Solomon, that is.

He had money, prestige, wisdom, and authority. And yet, he died unfulfilled. He describes himself as having searched the world over, had his way with all the women he wanted, met the most interesting people, and built the empire of his dreams. And despite being rich in all these ways, happiness and meaning seem to have escaped him.

Happiness has something to do with rich. But it's more about what you do with whatever degree of "rich" you find in your hands. That being the case, if it's really happiness you're after, as I suspect most of us actually are, then most likely it's already available to you even if your assessment of "rich" falls short of your ultimate goals and dreams.

Consider Solomon's conclusion: "God gives a man wealth, possessions and honor, so that he lacks nothing his heart desires, but God does not enable him to enjoy them... All man's efforts are for his mouth, yet his appetite is never satisfied."

There, on the page, is our very definition of rich as uttered by the man who is considered by many to have come the closest of anyone to experiencing it. Yet he reports what must have been a devastating discovery for him: "rich" does not equal "happy".

As much as it might seem off-topic to elaborate on this tangent, I feel an obligation to distinguish between the two. Otherwise, you might become rich forever in all the ways you imagine only to wonder why you weren't also happy forever, when in all likelihood you really meant to pursue *happy forever* in the first place.

It is a common misconception today that the only thing standing between us and our ultimate happiness is more "riches". We tell ourselves we'd pursue happiness more successfully if we had more resources with which to do so – if we had more finances, more freedom, or the ideal people to share it with. But Solomon would convince us otherwise. Indeed, he seems to be screaming from behind those ancient pages in an attempt to do just that. Though it may not be completely natural to identify with someone of Solomon's wealth, it would be unfortunate to overlook the similarities we share with him. He's not so different from you and me. And as we continue our own pursuit of happiness, Solomon offers us some vital information that can help us understand this idea of rich.

He was the richest man in history, yet one of the poorest in happiness.

Is it advisable, then, for us to press ahead believing that our lives will somehow be governed by different laws of nature? Can "rich" equal "happy" for us, even though it hasn't for thousands of years before we came along? Or should we learn from the advice of Solomon and Jesus, adding the vital component of transcendence to our recipe for happiness? For me, the personal ethos of generosity is the key to happiness and fulfillment.

While a full explanation of transcendence exceeds the scope of

> **The Law of Fulfillment states that we'll be fulfilled when we expend our time, talent, and treasure for the good of others.**

this book, I've concluded that it warrants a chapter here. To coin a phrase, I call it The Law of Fulfillment, which states that we'll be fulfilled when we expend our time, talent, and treasure for the good of others. For Solomon, it proved to be one of the few riddles he couldn't solve – a secret. And while it's not my goal to tell someone else how to live, I simply want to report that this has certainly turned out to be my own conclusion as well. You don't have to amass money to be rich. Nor is amassing money any guarantee of a rich experience once you do.

In closing, I'd like to explore one more angle to this idea of being rich forever. And just as the relationship between "rich" and "happy" has the potential to change everything, this final thought could make all the difference in the world.

Chapter 12

RICH FOREVER

"And everyone who has left houses or brothers or sisters or father or mother or wife or children or fields for my sake will receive a hundred times as much and will inherit eternal life."

Matthew 19:29 NIV

Throughout this book, it's been my goal to explore this idea of being rich from every conceivable angle. Frequently, that has meant rethinking some of the long-standing assumptions that shape our thoughts and guide our pursuits in life. The previous chapter gives a great example of one such assumption. I think it's important to verify some of these core foundations that form the basis of everything else we do. It may seem rather philosophical and abstract. But when you consider the tangible anguish and regret that torment all those who proceed innocently on their course in life only to meet with disappointment when it doesn't turn out like they expected, it suddenly becomes practical and real. There's nothing like working hard to come in first place, only to discover you've entered the wrong event. So when I examine my own desire to be rich forever, I strive to comprehend the relationship between all related ideas as much as possible – ideas like happiness, pleasure, and purpose. If a man like Solomon can miss it, none of us holds any guarantees.

In keeping with that practice, there's one more dimension to being "rich forever" I'd like to dissect. In this case, I'd like to challenge the "forever" part of the phrase. So exactly what does "forever" mean?

When we think of being rich some day, we're not talking about just for one day. We mean for all the days after as well. We mean forever. We don't think much about it, but we assume it's something that never ends, or maybe it goes on as long as the world, or maybe as long as our lives go on… or until the end of time. That's just it. What exactly does "forever" mean? And what if, in the spirit of transcendence, our personal forever lasts longer than other "forevers"? Do our riches transcend along with us? If we somehow manage to achieve the elusive state of "rich" – the one that involves transcendence – can it really last forever?

If we're ready to conclude that possessing riches can't make us happy, then we're basically suggesting that there's something about our existence that reaches beyond the things in the world around us. Indeed, the kind of happiness that resonates inside us can't be reproduced using only the ingredients we find in the visible universe. It seems to come only from a place that exists beyond the here and now. Even the term we've designated as our key to happiness – transcendence – alludes to things outside our own physical existence.

It would be one mistake to forge ahead with misconstrued assumptions about forever. But it would be another level of blunder altogether if we never develop our personal assumptions about it in the first place. So while I won't put myself up as an authority on the subject of eternity, I will issue a call to crystallize your own understanding of it as best you can.

Since most Americans surveyed say they believe in a higher power of some kind, I will approach this topic with a general tone of Judeo-Christian sentiment. If this context somehow misses you, I trust you'll be able to extract the main ideas and adopt them for your own with relative ease.

Of course, if you don't embrace the sort of belief that includes a life beyond this one, then this conversation is over before it begins. There's no need to consider other definitions of "forever". Your assignment is simply to develop a strategy that ensures riches to last your lifetime – including that sense of fulfillment that only transcendent pursuits can bring.

But if, like me, you think there's something to this concept of a Creator, and the Bible, and all the things they teach about eternity, then it stands to have a huge impact on our notion of "rich forever".

I'll leave the hard-core sermons to the professional preachers. Even so, where we land on the "forever" question has very practical implications on how we acquire, manage, and view our riches in this life. As I explained in Chapter 7, my beliefs have led me to set a limit – a maximum net worth I will ever accumulate for myself. Now, part of that decision was driven by the realization that beyond a certain point, dollars have their greatest value to me when applied toward transcendent things. However, I chose Christian charities because of what I've been taught about the kingdom that is to come. In short, Christianity suggests that this life is a mere foreshadowing of the eternal life that lies beyond the grave. Furthermore, it promises that we will be rewarded in the next life to the degree we invest our riches now toward that future kingdom. So you see, there's a very direct connection between what I do now and just how "forever" I should hope to be rich.

> **What if even simple acts of kindness store up eternal value? Can we possibly convert our lives in the here and now into eternal treasure?**

What if even simple acts of kindness store up eternal value? I'm not necessarily talking about giving money here. I'm thinking about how we spend our time, talent, and treasure. For example, when a young nurse volunteers after-hours to care for kids with cancer, what if her time is credited with some kind of eternal value? Or how about the simple act of buying a hot meal for a homeless man? Or even something as simple as spending an evening playing checkers with an elderly person in a nursing home? Of course, giving money to charity has a special place too. But what if these other ways of giving carry some sort of eternal currency value? Can we possibly convert our lives in the here and now into eternal treasure?

Now, I could present a long list of the passages behind these ideas.

But in short, let's just say there's a convincing theme connecting how you handle those things now – your time, talent, and treasure – and how rich you'll be in the future. Perhaps they are best summarized in these words, "Do not store up for yourselves treasures on earth, where moth and rust destroy, and where thieves break in and steal. But store up for yourselves treasures in heaven, where thieves do not break in and steal. For where your treasure is, there your heart will be also." Or when Jesus said, "And if anyone gives even a cup of cold water to one of these little ones because he is my disciple, I tell you the truth, he will certainly not lose his reward."

I imagine you're already familiar with verses like those above. Likewise, the basic concepts behind them aren't new either. The real question revolves around how literally we're supposed to take such things. On one hand, they provide a nice metaphor describing some helpful attitudes for everyone. But on the other hand, they might be viewed as literal instructions that should be measurable in our checkbook ledger. Which response is right? Literal, or metaphorical?

What if there really is another life after this one? And what if you really could be storing up riches to enjoy some day?

Essentially, the questions I'm raising are pretty fundamental: What if there really is another life after this one? And what if you really could be storing up riches to enjoy some day? Would it change the way you spend, save, and earn? Would it change the way you spend some of your time? Or your talent? Would you look at this idea of a "personal ethos of generosity" any differently? Or would you need more evidence before you'd go that far with it?

Fortunately, there's no real penalty for going with this theory. It's not an either/or proposition. If you store up treasures in heaven and you're beliefs prove to be right, then you truly have riches that will last forever. If however you store up treasures in heaven and the whole myth about God is debunked, you've still afforded yourself the fulfillment that comes from giving to something outside yourself. And presuming part of your contributions will help the needy and contribute to the good of all, those accomplishments are real regardless of what's true or untrue about the afterlife.

So in light of those possibilities, this choice has compelling advantages.

So which side do you favor? If it's true that your decisions with riches will have consequences for eternity, what opportunities does that suggest for you today? And if it doesn't – or if you're wrong – what do you really stand to lose?

In the worst case, you live the most fulfilling life you can live.

And in the best case?

You can be rich forever.

From the authors of the ground-breaking Blueprint for Life study

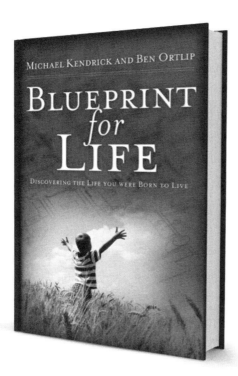

You were no accident.
Live your life *on purpose.*

You were God's idea. You were designed and equipped for a unique purpose in life. But what is that purpose? How can you find and pursue it? Blueprint for Life sets you on a journey to discover the life you were born to live!

For more information or to purchase, please visit blueprintforlife.com.

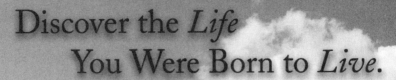